Construction Guide to Health and Wellbeing

Keeping Your Workers Well

Jane Coombs

DEDICATION

To John, always on hand to help with the

difficult maths and bringing me coffee.

Table Of Contents

Acknowledgements

Thanks to all my helpers and beta readers who helped make this book so much better and easier to understand.

My thanks as always to John (my husband), who knows almost as much as me now about occupational health and safety.

And my dear friend and colleague, Jackie Morris, who always comes up with the goods.

Thanks also to Sue Le Cuirot RGN SCPHN OH of Access Occupational Health Ltd., whose offer to help came unexpectedly and with it, some great suggestions.

Thanks to you all.

Introduction

My first exposure to construction was at age eight. I helped my uncle build a pigeon coop in the backyard. I held the block as he hammered the nails in; vibrations running up my arm as I bravely hung on. We were outside in our own private world for weeks it seems; it was probably only a couple of days. But on the day of the unveiling to the rest of the family, I was so proud of the angular gaping mouthed monster as my eyes feasted on the bits that I had done. What a feeling. I had a satisfying glow looking at the building, which we'd made from scraps of wood, nails, glue and then paint.

My dad and my brothers (I have five) worked in house building too, so it's always been a big part of my life. Wandering through skeleton houses and dangling from scaffold poles late at night.

Yes, I fully understand the appeal of the construction industry.

I have worked in the construction industry as a health professional, or should I say, around the edges of it, for many years, dealing with all levels of construction, from the one-man band 'subbie' like my uncle to the corporate giants like High Speed Two and Crossrail. I have written articles for magazines, blogs and books that cover general issues of construction.

And because construction is a unique proposition, I soon recognised the need for a reference book that gives managers, health and safety, HR and my colleagues in medicine insight into construction and how different it is due to temporary nature of workers. Because in other industries, the controlling body is always there (the employer) - it is permanent, whereas, in construction, management structures and responsibilities are built and when the project is finished - everyone and everything involved in the building tends to disappear. To accommodate this coming together of trades, the UK has had to construct a separate legal structure - the Construction Design and Management Regulations, which sit alongside the Health and Safety at Work Act applicable to other workplaces.

Read more in the first chapter and discover what a difference this makes to managing construction workers.

But it is more than just the law, and when I try to define why this is so, I struggle to pinpoint what the difference is – because, and there is no getting away from it, it is very different. The workers are down to earth, mostly funny and practical types. The work is usually dirty, dangerous, smelly, and leaves you exhausted. The projects are short lived as are your workmates who disappear overnight when the project finishes. Something I find tantalising.

I have written this book for anyone who works in construction and wants to:

1. Keep up to date on construction health issues
2. Know where to go for information
3. Access the reference sites the professionals use to organisations that provide or assist with construction health, and
4. Want to find out what all the fuss is about regarding managing the workforce

And for the record, and I say this here, loud and clear, I have very little technical knowledge on how to build a bridge or electrify a rail, but I do know what motivates workers, keeps them safe and healthy and where everyone in construction gathers for discussions about all of the above.

In this short reference book you will find the links and resources for everything health wise to do with construction - from the latest thinking on recruiting the disabled; to running your own health and wellbeing campaign. From putting health risks on your building information modelling (BIM) programme (*Chapter 5*) to getting the best type of health surveillance programme that conforms with all the government rules for tendering multi-billion pound projects (*Chapter 6*).

I've used everyday language, in a small book, both of which my uncle would appreciate. Keep it in your back pocket for quick advice on things that happen on a daily basis for issues such as where to get more information on things like silica exposures and where to go if you need an employee assistance programme (*Chapter 33.*)

There are also links to my website blog at <u>Working Well Solutions</u> (bit.ly/2skrreW) and my relevant videos where they add to understanding a complicated subject.

How to Use This Book

My book is not a storybook; although if you are new to construction or struggling to understand how it all works, I suggest you start at Chapter One, where you have the necessary information on how the construction cycle works. For the more experienced, look at the sections that interest you.

Keep the book handy when you get a query about health issues, such as:

- ◆ Where do I go to find out if I can get help with adaptations for workers who are disabled? *Chapter 35*
- ◆ Should I have a defibrillator (AED) on site? *Chapter 25*
- ◆ Who to contact about setting up an occupational health service? *Chapter 28*
- ◆ How can I take on a new worker without falling foul of discrimination laws? *Chapter 30*
- ◆ What is a toolbox talk? *Chapter 39*
- ◆ When and why you might need a hygienist? *Chapter 33*

I hope you find this book useful. It is an accumulation of all my time in construction, starting when I worked at Constructing Better Health and visited sites advising workers, managers, contractors and occupational health services on the best way of doing health in construction.

There is a huge interest in health now, especially after the figures show construction workers suicide rate is one of the highest occupational rates in the UK. *Chapter 26*

I am a qualified safety professional too, so you will notice that I have added the health elements in the context of safety strategy. In my mind, it is complicated to separate the two although some of my OH colleagues may disagree with me here.

The facts written in this book are correct at the time of publishing, however, with Brexit looming and changes happening, references may change. So, and I'm covering myself here, please check carefully any written facts and follow the links for more information. If the link doesn't work, then the chances are the data may have changed.

Links

In the book, words underlined are the direct links to website resources for the electronic book. If you have a print version of this book, you will see a shortened link, which usually starts with the letters 'bit'. Copy the full notation into your browser, and it will take you to the correct website.

For example, to visit my website, WorkingWellSolutions.com., copy and paste the following without the speech marks 'bit.ly/2skrreW' into your browser bar and it will take you there. It is a way of shortening the long tails of website addresses - they don't look pretty, and it's easy to make a mistake when trying to copy them!

I have written many articles and provide free templates on my website - <u>Working Well Solutions</u> (bit.ly/2skrreW), some of the downloads require registration for access.

More Books from Jane Coombs

If you need more information on either safety or health, try some of my other books:

- ♦ 'How to Look after the 'Elf in Health and Safety' (amzn.to/2sl2Fez)
- ♦ 'The Manager's Ultimate Guide to Health and Wellbeing at Work' (amzn.to/2skuwMe) both available on Amazon.

1. How Construction Works

If you have been in construction for years, you do not need to read this first chapter because I need to explain, to a layperson, how I see construction working. Be warned it is simplified and only for those new or considering starting a career in construction.

For those who have stayed, I will use an example of a Tesco's store to show how the supply chain and health and safety responsibilities work - but I could have used any other commissioning builder. Here goes.

A New Build

Tesco's want a new supermarket built, so (after buying the land, planning permission etc.,) they hire a designer or an architect to put the plans together. They hire people to do the job because Tesco does not employ builders or designers.

Tesco, now the 'client', (a legal term under the Construction Design and Management Regulations (bit.ly/2fnpnhb) (CDM) pays and oversees the work.

Tesco's draw up a contract containing everything they want from this new store, from the size of it, to lifespan, car parking spaces, customer toilets, and so on, and puts this out asking for bids from construction companies to build it as well as contract terms[1]. Several construction companies will bid to make the new Tesco and come up with a price for delivering what is required. When the bids come in Tesco looks at their submission for best value. A significant consideration when choosing the builder will be the quoted price, although elements of quality and timeframes are essential elements as well.

---

[1] *How to write a construction bid* (bit.ly/2rQ150W)

Tesco decides who has 'won' the contract, and the successful bid becomes the principal contractor or PC (another legal term under CDM) for the deal.

Usually, the principal contractor has to use other tradespeople to do small pieces of the build, like landscape gardening for the grounds or a plumber for all the pipework; they need diggers and ground investigation teams too. But as some tradesmen are only used on a small piece of work or for a limited time, they are not usually part of the principal contractor's workforce - you can imagine having a groundsman waiting around for the building to be finished before they can get in and plant those spiky shrubs. So many jobs are themselves put out to other companies to bid for, but this time it is the principal contractor, not the client, who takes control of the hiring process.

Second Tier Hiring

This second set of tendering for contracts is quite complex; calling for project managers, who coordinate everyone on behalf of the principal contractor. A small Tesco's would be quite easy to manage, but think how big the project might be for say the Olympic stadium.

The contract between each party (client, principal contractor and sub-contractors) has costs and delivery dates written in; if contractors fail to deliver on time, then the client can withhold money. Everyone works to clear deadlines set up by legal teams on both sides. And here is where the problems usually arise in health and safety terms, because safety and health procedures take time and extra money, which hasn't traditionally gone into the planning stages of the project. Health professionals can be expensive to hire, and medical checks take workers away from work, meaning that what little flexibility there may be in a project plan, quickly evaporates - especially with the usual problems that large builds throw in.

When the project is finished and the building handed over to Tesco, the PC and all the subbies, pack up and move on to another project.

Another complication, and where construction is massively different to any other industries, is that the majority of workers: the bricklayers, plant drivers, scaffolders, ground investigation, electricians, welders and visiting lorry drivers are NOT directly employed by the client or the PC. Their employer is based elsewhere, or the visiting workers are self-employed. There can also be sub sub sub-contractors, and these all form the so-called the tiers of construction.

Tiers of Construction

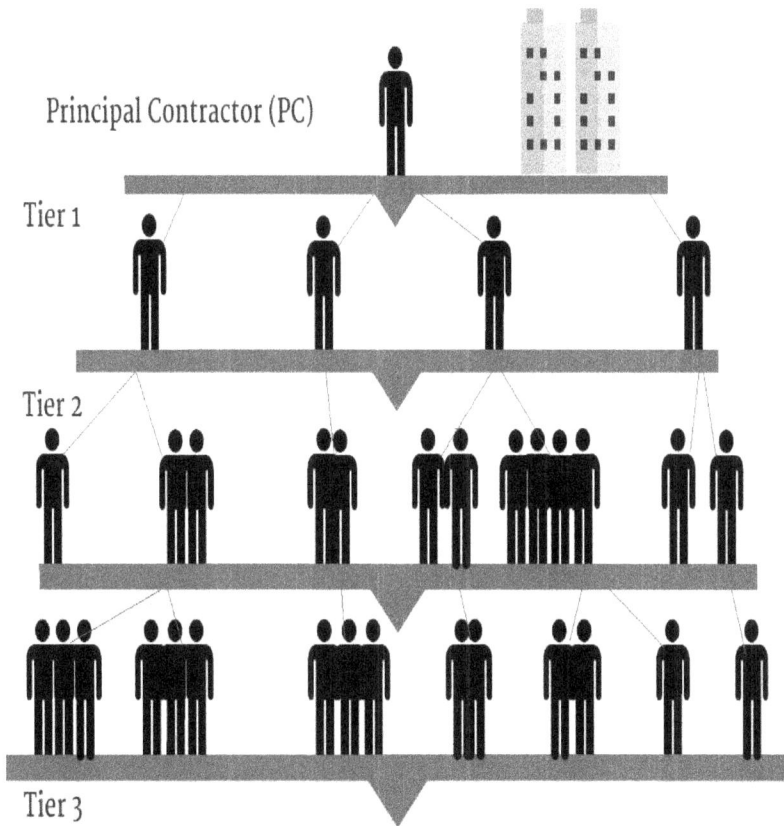

Principal Contractor (PC)

Tier 1

Tier 2

Tier 3

The PC is chosen as the successful bidder and wins the tender, who then has to decide who will do which parts of the build

The groups of workers work together and help each other. Usually, it all gels and has done for many years. Problems occur when the subcontractors or self-employed are asked to comply with a site-specific rule set by the principal contractor which may directly conflict with their distant employer who is managing the worker from afar. Here, the Health and Safety at Work Act comes into play which, in some cases, conflicts with the requirements of the CDM.

Let's say, for example, that the PC has written in the contract that each worker should have a safety critical medical before coming on site.

Joe's employer hasn't said this.

Joe is a lorry driver who is delivering some bricks; he is only on the site for a couple of hours. Should he still have a full medical? If so, who pays? What happens if he fails the medical? What if he doesn't have time for a medical check? By the time the PC or agent has gone into this, the delivery is done, and Joe has gone. And, things like this happen all the time - some much more severe, like Joe failing a site drug and alcohol test. He might be banned from one site but what is to stop him driving on the site down the road, where they don't do drug and alcohol testing?

So, the big issue in construction health and wellbeing is in managing the workers. You have new workers on site every day. Self-employed workers who may not want to comply with health procedures or who are afraid of admitting health issues for fear of being sent off-site. Worker's with unknown health risks and who are unlikely to tell you about their poor health. Also, they may not be safe to work, perhaps they are taking medication that affects alertness or should be home in bed but need the money? Add to that the current issue of the numbers of foreign and agency workers who barely understand the language, and you see the problem.

The PC is not the employer but must ensure everyone is fit for work; they are responsible for everyone on the site premises, and any actions affecting the neighbourhood, such as noise, dust and vibration from say, taking soil samples.

At the Olympics, the client provided health and safety induction, drug and alcohol testing and full medical provision for all workers, and the expense was enormous. Few construction companies can afford that.

Back to Tesco, who now have their shiny new store. The PC packs up and moves on to the next job to start the process all over again - but this time it's Thames Tideway or a new road.

Stop here and consider the logistics and mechanics of controlling a random group of tradespeople, all trying to get their work done and moving on to the next waiting job?

2. Why is Construction Different?

There are hundreds of health and safety laws applicable to work throughout all industries. What makes construction unique is the Construction Design and Management Regulations (CDM) which sits alongside the Health and Safety at Work Act.

1. Health and Safety at Work Act (HASAWA) (bit.ly/2F5EKBV): The HASAWA sets out duties for **all employ ers** in the UK, specifying that the employer should protect the health and safety of their employees and those affected by their work.

2. Construction Design and Management (CDM) Regulations: (bit.ly/2fnpnhb): CDM places legal duties on virtually everyone involved in construction work. Those with legal duties are 'duty holders'.

The 2007 regulations sets out a principal designer to replace the CDM coordinator whose job it was to tackle health and safety issues at the design stage rather than wait until the building is underway.

On construction sites, the primary duty holder is the principal contractor (PC) who has duties to protect the health of those on site. Note - the **PC is not usually the employer.**

CDM aims to improve health and safety in the industry by helping to:

- ♦ Sensibly plan the work, so the risks involved are managed from start to finish
- ♦ Have the right people for the right job at the right time
- ♦ Cooperate and coordinate work with others
- ♦ Have the correct information about the risks and how they are being managed
- ♦ Communicate this information efficiently to those who need to know
- ♦ Consult and engage with workers about the hazards and how they are controlled

These two overarching laws sometimes conflict because of the duties of employers to their workers, as opposed to the legal responsibilities of the client, principal contractor and subcontractors on a site.

As you have seen, construction projects are finite. They have a beginning and end. Whether it is a bridge or shop or a railway, there has to be an entity to manage it and a workforce to make it. Someone has to take responsibility and be 'in charge', as many of the workers on site are generally not the employees of the company making the structure - he or she does their bit and moves on. The managing bodies of the building move on too, but the **employer** of the workers is based, and remains based in, say, Sheffield.

The purpose of the CDM Regulations is to allocate responsibilities and duties so that workers or the public are not injured or hurt; this identifies accountabilities at every stage and for each function. If there is an incident, there are also provisions in both the laws mentioned above for blame and retribution (that is, compensation for injury caused).

As you read through this book, apply the principles of construction projects in the context of the example above, and you will begin to grasp the complexity of managing different and complex health issues on a grand scale.

Further Advice and Resources

♦ HSE has published <u>Legal Series guidance</u> that supports CDM (bit.ly/2rQppzF) with more detail
♦ A <u>video on CDM</u> (bit.ly/2pBfjVy) and other linked issues
♦ HSE website <u>New to Health and Safety in Construction</u> (bit.ly/2rTCBnD)
♦ <u>Managing Health and Safety in Construction</u> (bit.ly/2pBpKbu), a free download from the HSE
♦ <u>Managing Contractors</u> (bit.ly/2sPL3ET) a brief guide
♦ <u>CDM Regulations Factsheet</u> (ubm.io/2fuKQVk) from SHP Online

3. General Health and Work

Why Health Is Difficult to Understand

Many managers ask why health at work is so important. What is so different from normal health at home or health on holiday? The answer is that it is unethical and immoral to injure workers health in order to make profits; therefore, society has legislated that businesses must protect the health of the workers. What workers do in their own time is their choice. But what is also true is that when a company makes a profit without safeguarding workers from harm - that is not right.

The problem that managers' face when trying to protect health at work is that health is complicated--not straightforward, instant, and logical like mathematics, where if you add one and one together they always equal two.

Health issues remain rife in the construction industry, whereas safety problems are mainly under control. And although there is still work to do, the accident and fatality rate has lessened over the years.

Now, however, we see some startling facts about health, which Park Health call the 'slow accidents', such as cancers and disabling skin problems. These health issues come about sometimes years after exposure, but we know this, and how to prevent these; construction can start to tackle the beginnings of any health effect.

Effects on the Body

Things that affect the body enter through various methods: by breathing in toxins, through absorption via the skin and mucous membranes, inoculation (think syringes) and ingestion (eating with contaminated hands). The environment too has a massive impact on the body from noise, light, vibration, and heat etc.

Health effects are difficult to monitor due to the silent nature of health. Problems may be silently cooking away to emerge years

8

later; in some, there will be no visible effect until it is too late to do anything about it.

There are three types of reactions to consider for health issues:

3.1 Immediate/Acute Health Reactions (e.g., carbon monoxide):

+ Occurs suddenly
+ The bad effect appears within seconds to hours of exposure
+ Usually, there is an easily identifiable cause
+ May follow repeated or prolonged exposure to a health hazard
+ May lead to the worker being removed from the hazard and/or seeking early medical attention

For the immediate or acute effect, workers are quickly ill and removed from the hazard. In my experience, these reactions become well known in the business and prompt immediate action. No one wants to work with materials that injure health so badly and obviously.

3.2 Delayed Effects (e.g., lung cancer):

+ Occurs hours to years after the exposure
+ The person affected may not link it to a specific hazard or workplace
+ May not have visible signs of ill health or effect until it's too late to do anything about it
+ May only be found through health checks or sophisticated hospital testing

3.3 Chronic Effects (e.g., asbestosis):

+ Occurs gradually over an extended period of time (often years)
+ May not be readily diagnosed or linked to a specific hazard

♦ Does not result in immediate action by employer to correct as the worker may not connect the health problem with work of years before

Delayed or chronic effects may need identification by experts such as occupational health or hygienists (see Chapter 33); they can advise at the health needs assessment stage.

If you are going to do the health risk assessment yourself, you must understand what affects health and the difference between a health and a safety risk assessment otherwise; risk assessment tends to be all about safety with little about health.

This sounds simple enough, but is it?

Not Straightforward

Health in individuals is not straightforward. Its affected by many individual characteristics, such as age, genetics, behaviour, gender, ethnicity, past medical health, nurture, etc., so predicting health outcomes can be highly sophisticated.

Not Instant

With safety issues there is no time delay--someone slips in a puddle and whoops! The worker has a sprained ankle or broken leg. Instant! Clear up the water, investigate and rectify, retrain the workers, and fill in an accident form and the incident is less likely to happen again.

With health issues, there is often a considerable time delay from the time of exposure to the effect.

Take asbestos workers. Work started back in the 1960s and 1970s with no protection or advice against the deadly asbestos fibres. Yet I am sure if managers (and society) knew what the effects of asbestos were then, they would have been more eager to protect workers. If everyone who had worked with asbestos had suddenly developed a hacking cough and gone off sick, society would have begun to inquire as to the reasons. However, the hacking cough and cancers took forty years to develop, and today we are dealing with the fallout.

Many health problems are slow moving and the effects delayed. But we know that now so we can better deal with health risks by having laws such as COSHH - Chapter 3 and RIDDOR see Chapter 7. Because uncontrolled health issues can sabotage attendance rates and staff turnover, assist claimants against your company, and even take profits through prosecution, fees for intervention, and personal claims.

Further Advice and Resources

- Guidance on COSHH (bit.ly/2tVdn8v) from the HSE
- Guidance on RIDDOR (bit.ly/2tUPkXc) from the HSE

Health Effects in Construction

Different jobs in construction have risks, which, if not eliminated or controlled, cause harm to the individual. Protecting the health of workers is the responsibility of the employer and site principal constructor; which is why most large or high-risk organisations engage medical services to advise management on compliance, best practice and initiate general health programmes that make good business sense (e.g., wellbeing, attendance management programmes).

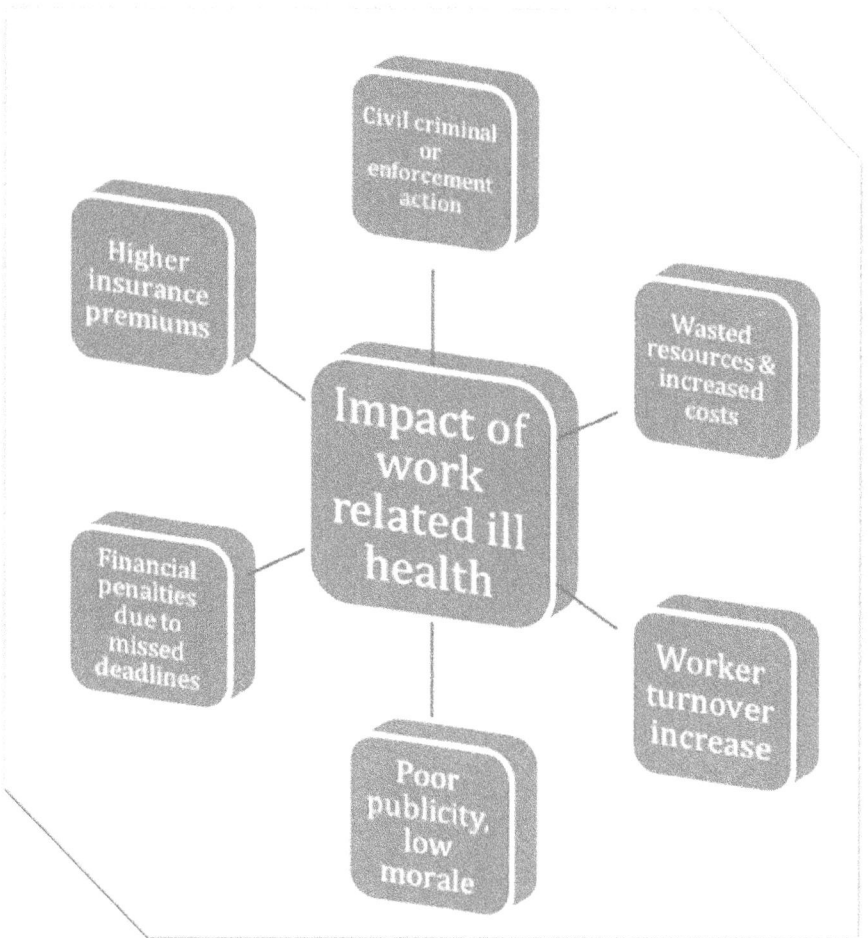

As for health management generally, evidence from the Health and Safety Executive (HSE) show a higher number of deaths occur from people who have contracted a disease through years of exposure to uncontrolled health risks than those injured at work. By not understanding or controlling health risks at work, employers contribute to the national burden on health services, individual pain and suffering and reduce potential profits from prosecution and poor performance, as well as bad publicity.

On-Site Health

Sub-contractors or agency workers arriving on a construction site fall into one of three categories when it comes to being fit for work:

1. Most are perfectly fit to do their job yet there is no proof of it
2. Some will have had full health checks and clearance from a previous post
3. A minority may have serious health problems which they will not want to declare

To address the health issues and ensure workers are fit for the job, more extensive construction projects tend to set up site-based health checking services.

Each worker fills in a full health questionnaire and will have a number of medical tests depending on their job.

Characteristics of Construction Workers

Construction workers have complex health issues that interfere with applying the law and protecting their health - here are some:

- Many are subcontractors and self-employed, there is no 'employer', and they do not to want to spend time or money having health checks
- It is a male-dominated workforce which traditionally does not visit the doctor

- Many work away from their home with little support from friends and family
- Will not be registered with a GP local to where they work
- May not be paid if they don't work
- Workers pay depends on how much work they do, that is, piecework
- Projects are rarely in a permanent location

From a health and safety perspective, there is a massive input into construction workers training and capability. Here are the main issues that need to cover the workforce:

- Induction programmes
- Personal protective clothing which complies with regulations
- Fitness for work
- Ability to do the job
- When and where they will arrive on site
- Welfare and eating facilities
- First Aid provision
- Drug and alcohol testing
- Different groups of workers such as young, non-English speaking, pregnant, disabled

The most common health issues in construction result in:

1.1 Cancers

3700 deaths per year due to working with asbestos (70%), silica (17%) painters using and removing paint with lead in, and diesel exhaust fumes

1.2 Exposure to Hazardous Substances

Dust, chemicals and harmful mixtures, fumes, vapours or gases in the air causes breathing problems and lung diseases. Skin disease in the form of dermatitis is also prevalent.

1.3 Physical Issues

- ♦ Back injuries and upper limb disorders. Manual handling is the most commonly reported injury in the industry
- ♦ Vibration and Noise (see Chapters 8 and 10)

1.4 Other

New problems are emerging relating to mental health. All of which will need addressing.

Construction Response

Health is high on the agenda for construction; recognising that workers' health has been ignored. Now there are new initiatives:

- ♦ IOSH Cancer campaign: No Time to Lose (bit.ly/2sdmlwu)
- ♦ HSE: Managing Occupational Health Risks in Construction (bit.ly/2pSJ6J0)
- ♦ BOHS: Breathe Freely (bit.ly/2rcpZYe)

Yet even with all this focus on health, a report in May 2017, from the Building Safety Group (bit.ly/2rGfVXT) points out there was an 18% increase in site health breaches after 10,000+ independent inspections over the preceding four-month period.

The main issues being:

- ♦ Dust and fume infringements (up 43%),
- ♦ Breaches of noise limits (up 23%)
- ♦ COSHH violations (up 17%)

There is still a long way to go.

Further Advice and Resources

- ♦ Finding a GP (bit.ly/2tyQPdy)

4. Health Needs Assessment (HNA)

So where and how do you start assessing health risks on your site?

The answer is to do a health needs assessment, which is a normal risk assessment, but the focus on health (rather than safety), taking into account people's responses and susceptibility to health hazards.

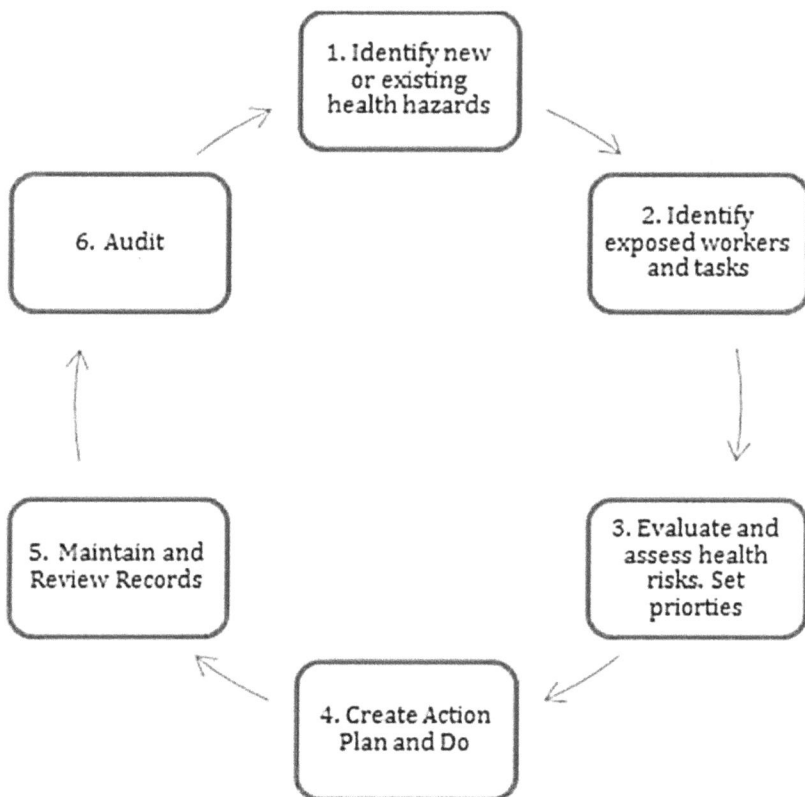

```
          ┌──────────────┐
          │ 1. Identify new │
          │   or existing   │
          │ health hazards  │
          └──────────────┘
  ┌──────────┐              ┌──────────────┐
  │ 6. Audit │              │ 2. Identify    │
  │          │              │ exposed workers│
  └──────────┘              │   and tasks    │
                            └──────────────┘
  ┌──────────────┐          ┌──────────────┐
  │ 5. Maintain and │        │ 3. Evaluate and │
  │ Review Records  │        │  assess health  │
  └──────────────┘          │   risks. Set    │
                            │   priorties     │
          ┌──────────────┐  └──────────────┘
          │ 4. Create Action │
          │   Plan and Do    │
          └──────────────┘
```

Who Should Do a HNA

For many businesses, health risks from processes are well-known, and there is lots of free information available from the HSE or trade bodies. However, for those who work in high-risk or novel environments, or exposed to substances that severely affect the body, further investigation may be required.

In construction, someone who understands the principles of health management and has experience of the health hazards on a typical construction site, should lead or at the least, be consulted, about the health needs assessment and the type of medical support available for construction businesses.

When to Do an HNA

To save time and expense, do your health needs assessment at the earliest stage of a project or operations, review it periodically, and revisit when there is a significant change or as required by legislation. That way, you can allow for health monitoring and surveillance at the tendering stage of the process.

Identify New or Existing Health Hazards

Health hazard identification considers all facets of work activity, in order to identify potential health hazards.

Begin by considering the process of how you do your business. Are there substances, practices, or procedures that have health risks?

Are there naturally occurring health hazards (e.g., radon and sunlight)? Does the work involve asbestos, lead, compressed air, or ionising radiation? Is the work environment hot or cold and will that have an impact on workers? What sort of equipment is used? You'll find a wealth of information on the HSE website. Ask manufacturers about their products they supply and request safety data sheets.

What Increases or Decreases the Health Risk?

Consider these factors:

- ♦ The length of exposure: how long does a worker work with the hazard - all day or just a few minutes? The longer the exposure, the more likely it is they will have a problem

- Level of exposure: what kind of work are they doing? Are they in close contact or merely supervising workers who are? For example, engineers usually have more exposure to hazardous substances than say a supervisor
- Mode of exposure (e.g., direct contact, inhalation, injection, or ingestion): consider how the harm occurs (e.g., ground workers may get needle stick injuries from used syringes)
- Individual differences: such as age, height, sex, habits, e.g., people who smoke increase their risk from asbestos and vibration white finger)
- Contact with hazard (e.g., hand applying, spraying, remote pumping)
- Work environment--the layout of the area may make the activity more hazardous (e.g., incorrect height, inadequate ventilation or lighting, confined space)
- The season or environmental conditions such as hot/cold
- Review all workplace activity, including routine and non-routine tasks and emergency activities. Conducting a "real-time" observation of working practices may reveal surprises!
- Remember to ask workers what problems they have.

Here is a list of issues that may influence health:

Geographical location

- Temperature and climate (e.g., extreme heat or cold) and wide temperature variations
- Humidity and air quality
- Daylight (extremes of dark or light)
- Transport
- Communication infrastructure (emergency rescue)
- The nearest hospital (distance and access)
- Standard of health-care facilities
- Security (e.g., stress, anxiety, violence)

Physical

- Noise
- Motion (e.g., sea sickness)
- Vibration (e.g., hand-arm, whole body)
- Pressure (e.g., vessels, diving, tunnelling)
- Ionising and non-ionising radiation (e.g., sun exposure)
- Thermal work environment (e.g., tunnelling)
- Display screen equipment to include dashboard and feedback screens
- Ergonomics: associated with mismatches between the task and capability (including manual handling, repetitive movements)
- Equipment, especially if poorly designed, is used correctly, or it malfunctions. Consider:

  - Condition and age (newer equipment has less wear and tear)
  - Maintenance programmes and calibrations
  - Specific health hazards linked to the processes (e.g., noise, vibration, radiation, heat, cold, and exhaust emissions)
  - Training and method of use

- Sharp objects
- Transport at work

Technical assistance may be required to objectively measure physical hazards (e.g., vibration, dust levels), and if the results of measurements are within legal, published, or industry-accepted limits.

Chemical (usually covered in COSHH risk assessment)

- Poisons that accumulate in the body (e.g., heavy metals, lead)
- Irritants (cause a local effect on the skin, eyes, or lungs)

- Sensitisers (cause skin and breathing reactions, such as rash or asthma)
- Acids and alkalis/caustic agents
- Cancer-causing agents (e.g., diesel exhaust fume)
- Characteristics of the harmful agent (What is the size of the molecule in fume, smoke, dust? How far will the molecule travel in the lung?)

For substances supplied by third parties or manufacturers, look at safety data sheets (SDS) (bit.ly/2s1KzuZ). These contain the scientific information on a material purchased from a supplier; also ask for the SDS for specific use or processes.

Consider the most current information from SDSs, industry trade groups, national health and safety bodies, add and review the current scientific levels of exposure limits and make sure they are not exceeded. If in any doubt about the contents or the meaning of the SDS, contact the supplier for more information.

Biological (usually covered in COSHH risk assessment)

- Wildlife (e.g., animals including pets and guard dogs, reptiles, insects, plants)
- Endemic/epidemic diseases (due to viruses, bacteria, fungi, parasites)
- Contaminated food and drink
- Poor hygiene (due to catering, accommodation, toilet facilities, waste disposal)

Psychosocial (usually covered by stress risk assessments)

- Isolation (degree of access to social support)
- Overcrowding and lack of privacy
- Communication problems (business and family contact for those working away from home for long periods)
- Discrimination
- Bullying and harassment

- Culture, local laws, religion, and language (e.g., comprehension and comfort level)
- Job design (e.g., control, workload)
- Job organisation (e.g., shift patterns, sleep deprivation, rotations, jet lag)
- Leisure and recreation opportunities
- Substance abuse/dependence, alcohol use and addiction, and smoking
- Beliefs and culture of your workforce

Individual Characteristics (usually assessed by health professionals)

- Health status--in the case of psychological hazards, domestic and relationship pressures may affect an individual's ability to handle workplace stress
- Beliefs/motivators
- Demographics (e.g., age, sex, gender)
- Learning ability (e.g., dyslexia, reading ability, understanding)
- What tablets or medications an individual takes, for example, diabetics on insulin must eat at certain times, or they could become unconscious
- Personality (e.g., compliant, attitude to risk)
- Physical condition (e.g., obese, fit)
- Hobbies/lifestyle (e.g., those who go clubbing, listen to loud music or rifle shooting may already have problems with their hearing before they begin work)

The lists are not exhaustive. Identifying the hazards will determine the hazard profile for any activity. More information may be needed for individual workers who already have a health issue (rather than the group).

Reducing the Risk: Control Methods and Remedial Actions

As the HNA progresses, collect information and review the health issues, it is crucial to consider control and remedial actions as you go along. This method becomes a productive health exercise in itself- allowing high and medium risks to be minimised.

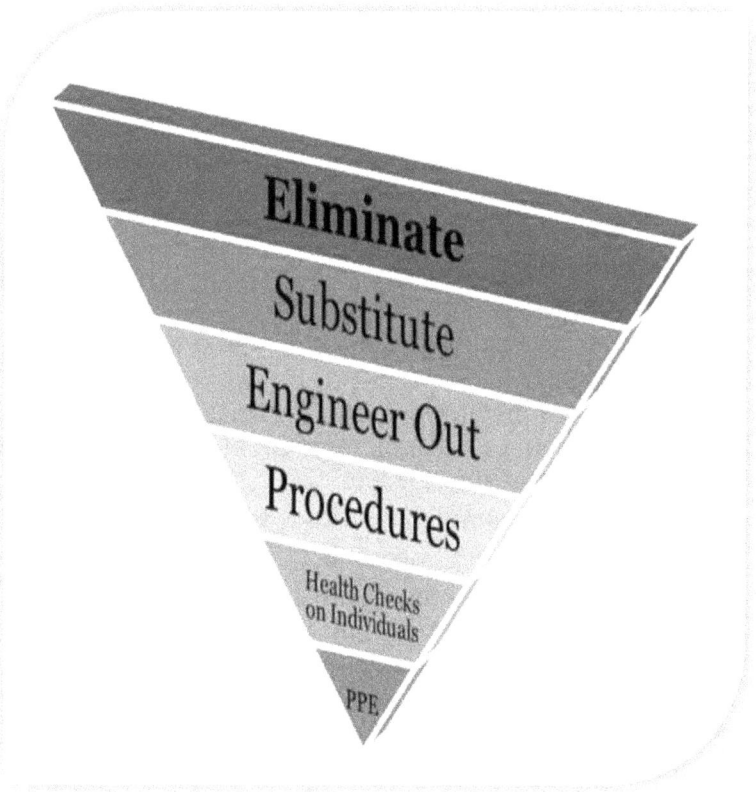

Eliminate
Substitute
Engineer Out
Procedures
Health Checks on Individuals
PPE

Hierarchy of Control for Health Risks

The general principles of controlling adverse exposure to hazards; known as the hierarchy of control, which is a priority list of the most effective means of reducing risk. The least effective means of control mean they are easily overridden or are dependent on human behaviours, thus not foolproof.

The hierarchy of control is the six ways of controlling health risks. This diagram shows that the first priority is to remove the material/process. If it is not possible to eliminate; work down through the pyramid until you get to the last, and least efficient method, which is using personal protective equipment (PPE).

Eliminate:

Do you need to do this part of the process or could you outsource this part of the work to avoid health risks?

Substitute:

Use a less hazardous substance or process, for example, using water-based paints instead of solvent-based paints.

Engineer Out:

Modify the equipment or process to cut down on the potential for danger (e.g., use local exhaust ventilation or containment, build a barrier to contain fumes or gases to protect workers from contamination); many now use local exhaust ventilation to collect construction dust at the source of contact.

Procedures:

Provide written safe working practices and in-house standards for control of exposure, sometimes called safe operating procedures (SOPs) or method statements. In some cases, there may be sufficient information available for employers to set an in-house working standard (e.g., information from manufacturers and suppliers of the substance or from publications of industry associations and occupational medicine and hygiene journals).

Also included in this step is education and training--all those who work with hazards should have training, explaining how to protect themselves. Training programmes may be required for supervisors regarding the identification of health risks.

See also Tool Box Talks, Chapter 39

Health-Checking Programmes:

Health-checking programmes involve asking or testing workers to make sure there are no ill effects from the work they do. You are verifying your control methods are working plus identifying susceptible workers. If some workers are even slightly affected, this leads to a review of the health risk assessment and tighter control methods.

Health checks are also used to make sure that individuals are fit to do their job and do not present a problem to themselves or a danger to others or the public; for example, those who erect scaffold or drive heavy plant machinery.

Personal Protective Equipment (PPE):

As you can see PPE is at the very bottom of the control methods to consider because workers have to understand how to use PPE and the protection provided. They can choose to ignore the gloves whereas the other ways are difficult to override or ignore. In cases where workers have suffered ill health effects, PPE was insufficient for the hazard, faulty, contaminated, or worn incorrectly.

Pay particular attention to how you introduce new control and remedial measures because these could be hazardous in other ways. For example, PPE can add an additional risk of even more heat in extreme heat situations; the PPE can stop heat escaping from the body or cause safety spectacles to steam up and reduce vision.

Also, consider:

- Welfare provision
- Making changes to policies, arrangements, or responsibilities
- Obtaining technical assistance (e.g., toxicologist, ergonomists, hygienists) to manage and control risks identified and to give professional advice
- Engaging an occupational health service provider for health checks on workers if required

Further Advice and Resources

- For PPE in the context of construction go to Chapter 23. For more information download the personal protective equipment (bit.ly/2tG14N4) Approved Code of Practice
- HSG 65 (bit.ly/2pCBDOs), a model management system and how health concerns fit into the overall management of risk
- Provision of welfare facilities (bit.ly/2vNpQyJ) HSE
- Health Needs Assessment from Public Health England (bit.ly/2xpDt8)

5. Building Information Modelling (BIM)

When designing or planning a new building or structure, its common nowadays to use a computer software programme commonly referred to as building information modelling or BIM.

There are many definitions of BIM, such as:

♦ A software package
♦ A 3D virtual model of buildings
♦ A process
♦ The organisation of all building data into a database so that it can answer questions in both a 'visual' and a 'numerical' way

It is safe to say that BIM is all the above and some more. It is a 3D digital model of a building or structure that shows all the steps of building and simulation of the building, part by part, long before construction starts.

Everyone involved in the build has access to their essential information, meaning that clients, building owners and operators get access to each stage of the project (if required).

A HSE study found that in 43 percent of the construction accidents, designers failed to address hazards leading up to the incident. One way to improve the design stage of a project is through BIM where many health risks can be 'designed out'.

The safety aspects of buildings have always been a part of a designers remit with safety hazards marked in red hazard boxes on plans. But very little has been done in respect of health hazards - yet there are many ways of reducing health risks at the planning and design stage.

Examples of designing out health risks:

- ◆ Remove drilling, grinding and cutting processes and reducing dust production
- ◆ Off-site assembly of component parts
- ◆ Increased use of mechanisation to mitigate the chances of, say, bad backs.

All UK government construction projects must use BIM now.

BIM and Health Risks

BIM provides a new opportunity to add health as well as safety risks to a planned project; the only problem may be that designers and architects may not have the training to understand the types of health risks.

I have put together a table of possible health risks in construction and where they may occur. See Appendix 3 for the full table - but bear in mind it is a starting point. The columns are self-explanatory.

Use the matrix for an overview of health issues and add your own as your projects progress. Managers, architects, planners and engineers can use this table of health risks as a starting point for considering how they can 'design out' these risks, before the threat occurs, ensuring workers health is protected at all stages, whether construction, maintenance or decommissioning.

Further Advice and Resources

- ◆ See BIM YouTube video (bit.ly/2rEtbPV)
- ◆ Download Health Risks matrix directly from my website Working Well Solutions/BIM (bit.ly/wws-com)

6. Legally Required Medicals

Workers exposed to asbestos, lead, ionising radiation, compressed air or substances listed in Schedule 6 of the Control of Substances Hazardous to Health Regulations (bit.ly/1g9ficD) (COSHH) may need specially trained and registered medical professionals, called, Appointed Doctors for supervising their health.

Appointed Doctors

Appointed Doctors (AD) are doctors who advise on specific health issues linked to work, e.g. lead or compressed air. AP's have to attend training and keep up to date with the regulations relating to the health risk, e.g., Control of Lead at Work Regulations (bit.ly/2rIbTy3). Doctors in this category have duties to the employee, employer and to the HSE and must have a full understanding of work processes to be able to apply their knowledge.

Asbestos

Exposure to asbestos-containing materials is the single most significant health risk in construction today; in the UK 20 tradesmen a week, are dying due to past exposure, with those working in refurbishment and demolition of existing buildings at most risk.

There are four diseases associated with asbestos work:

- Mesothelioma (bit.ly/2v2ka3u) which is always fatal
- Lung cancer (bit.ly/2v21lgV) almost always lethal
- Asbestosis (bit.ly/2v25KjN) not always fatal, but debilitating
- Diffuse pleural thickening is not fatal

Most asbestos work (including all work with sprayed asbestos, coatings, asbestos insulation or lagging and most work with asbestos insulating board) requires a licence from the HSE, due to the hazardous nature of these materials. It only works where the risk of exposure is low (such as work with asbestos cement) that is not ordinarily licensable.

Symptoms of asbestos illness can develop up to 60 years after exposure, which is why we have so many deaths now.

History of Asbestos

Asbestos was a widely used material in commercial buildings, homes and machinery until banned in 1999. What many people don't understand is that asbestos, because of its use, is now actually in the air in low concentrations. However, working directly with asbestos-containing materials (ACM's) can give personal exposures to airborne asbestos that is much higher than average environmental levels. Repeated work with asbestos increases your chance of developing a health problem later on in life. But, if the correct measures are in place and workers understand the risk, then there is little likelihood of a health problem.

Asbestos Law

Because of the health risks and public concern when working with asbestos, there are stringent regulatory controls on its use, achieved through the licensing of work. In addition, in the updating of the Regulations in 2012, non-licensed work now requires notification of work, and medical surveillance by a GP.

Employers must measure the number of asbestos fibres in the air when working with it.

There are two measures to take; one is a long-term measurement;

The long-term control limit for asbestos is 0.1 asbestos fibres per cubic centimetre of air (0.1 f/cm³).

The other is short duration defined within regulations to mean any one person working for less than one hour, or more than one person working for less than two hours in any seven consecutive days.

The control limit is not a 'safe' level, and exposure from work activities involving asbestos must be reduced to as far below the control limit as possible. Hygienists (see Chapter 33), can be used to measure and advise on safe practices.

As well as sticking to the regulations and guidance, employers must also provide training for workers on the following:

- Fitting and wearing of face masks
- Safe methods of working
- Dealing with asbestos waste

Licensed work is generally linked to regular work with asbestos or significant exposure to the fibres. In these cases, employers should:

- Notify the appropriate authority responsible for the asbestos work site.
- Mark the work area.
- Write specific asbestos procedures, such as standard operating procedures and a safe system of work.
- Arrange for employees to have medical surveillance (regular health checks) by an appointed doctor
- When and how to report any concerns

Training for Workers

Inform workers of the risks of breathing in fibres through training programmes; encourage them to stop smoking, as this contributes to the adverse health effects of asbestos exposure.

Smoking alone can cause lung cancer. Asbestos exposure alone can also cause lung cancer. Asbestos and smoking, taken together, multiply the risk of lung cancer significantly.

Further Advice and Resources

- The Control of Asbestos Regulations (bit.ly/2rKAyCf) is the primary law
- The HSE Asbestos microsite (bit.ly/2rHJ98H) offers free advice
- Licensable work with Asbestos (bit.ly/2rKh4gN) from the HSE
- Non-licensed asbestos work (bit.ly/2rKLsrA) with flow chart
- 'No Time to Lose' (bit.ly/2sdmlwu) IOSH Cancer campaign
- Asbestos and health effects information (bit.ly/2rKIS4O) from the NHS
- Beware Asbestos from HSE (bit.ly/2rKx02X) A free App - takes you through the steps of identifying and dealing with asbestos

Videos and Images

- Asbestos manufacture and use - the Evil Dust (bit.ly/2rKnkFj)
- Lung disease due to asbestos, how the fibres cause damage (bit.ly/2rKUS6k)
- HSE image gallery showing photographs of typical asbestos-containing materials found in buildings today (bit.ly/2rKpo0o)

Lead

The Control of Lead at Work Regulations (bit.ly/2rIbTy3) set out employers' duties, which are two-fold:

1. To protect the health of workers by preventing (or where this is not reasonably practicable, adequately controlling) exposure to lead.
2. To monitor the amount of lead absorbed by workers, so that individuals whose work involves significant exposure

to lead can stop work that is putting them in danger before their health is affected.

Any work which produces lead dust, fume or vapour can affect construction workers health most notably in the following types of work:

♦ Blast removal and burning of old lead paint
♦ Stripping of old lead paint from doors, windows etc
♦ Hot cutting in demolition and dismantling operations
♦ Painting of buildings
♦ Working with metallic lead and alloys containing lead, e.g. soldering
♦ Using pigments, colours and ceramic glazes

Lead enters the body when items holding lead are processed, worked, or recovered from scrap or waste. The dust created can be absorbed when:

♦ Breathing in lead dust, fume or vapour
♦ Swallowing any lead, e.g. during eating, drinking or smoking, biting nails without washing hands and face

Any lead absorbed will circulate in the blood; and some will stay in the body, stored mainly in bones and, remaining there for many years without any adverse effects.

If the level of lead gets too high, it can cause symptoms such as headaches and tiredness, and continued exposure could cause kidney, nerve and brain damage plus infertility.

An unborn child is at particular risk from exposure to lead, especially in the early weeks.

Appointed doctors monitor those at risk from lead by taking blood and urine samples and testing lead levels.

For most employees, if the amount of lead in the blood sample taken by the doctor reaches 50 µg/dl-called the action level-the employer must investigate and try to reduce the level.

If, despite all the control measures, blood-lead levels reach 60 µg/dl-called the suspension level-the doctor will advise on stopping work with lead. An employer must act on a doctors' decision, and the employee will not be able to work with lead again until it is safe to do so.

The table below sets out the action level (that is, the level employers need to do something) and suspension level (when a worker can no longer work with lead).

Category	Action Level	Suspension Level
General workers	**50 µg/dl**	**60 µg/dl**
Women of child-bearing age	**25 µg/dl**	**30 µg/dl**

Employers are obliged to:

♦ Risk-assess work with lead and minimise the amount of time spent working with it
♦ Adopt safe systems of work, install engineering controls such as dust, and fume extraction
♦ Train employees on how to protect themselves
♦ Provide washing and changing facilities and places free from lead contamination for eating
♦ Inform employees about risks to health from lead and necessary precautions to take

The law gives greater protection to young people under 18 and women capable of having children; they are barred from working in lead smelting and refining as well as from most jobs that manufacture lead-acid batteries.

Further Advice and Resources

♦ The <u>Control of Lead at Work Approved Code of Practice and Guidance</u> (bit.ly/2t59LkM) is available as a free download

Compressed Air

There are various types of health problems caused by working in a pressurised atmosphere such as tunnelling. The most common are:

♦ <u>Decompression sickness</u> (bit.ly/2tQyDfE)
♦ Barotrauma principally affecting the ears and sinuses
♦ Dysbaric osteonecrosis, a long-term, chronic condition damaging the long bone (hip or shoulder) joints

The main type of work is during tunnelling and other construction work in compressed air. As well as the standard safety provision there is a duty on employers to provide health surveillance via an Appointed Doctor.

Further Advice and Resources

♦ <u>The Work in Compressed Air Regulations</u> (bit.ly/2t4V3u1)

Radiation

There are two main kinds of radiation relevant to construction; ionising (that which requires statutory health surveillance) and non-ionising, both of which may cause harmful health effects.

Ionising radiation:

♦ From naturally <u>occurring radon gas</u> (bit.ly/2BleIci); some geographical areas have higher levels of radon than others
♦ Radiography or from thickness measuring gauges

Excess doses of ionising radiation can cause burns, sickness and have other adverse health effects.

Further Advice and Resources

- ◆ See Ionising Radiations Regulations 1999 (bit.ly/2slGWU5)
- ◆ Guidance from the HSE on health and safety (bit.ly/2slnEy3) aspects.

Non-Ionising Radiation:

Lasers can cause burns and damage the eye. Ultra-violet (UV) radiation (e.g. from the sun) can damage the skin and lead to skin cancer, particularly relevant in summer when construction workers traditionally shed their clothes.

Too much sunlight is harmful to the skin. Some medicines can also make skin more sensitive to sunlight.

Longer-term problems from sun exposure can increase the chance of developing skin cancer.

A recent study[2] showed that construction workers had the highest number of deaths (44% of deaths), followed by agriculture workers (23% of deaths).

As sun exposure can happen at work or at home, it has not generally been considered a work-related health risk, although with numbers of people with skin cancers increasing, this approach is now changing.

See also Chapter 24 for cancers related to construction.

---

[2] Youngson, A. (2017). Sun exposure at work could lead to one skin cancer death a week. [online] Www3.imperial.ac.uk. [Accessed 1 Aug. 2017].

7. RIDDOR

Many people know that you have to report accidents to the HSE. But did you know that you have to report certain work-related industrial diseases as well?

Employers and the self-employed must report diseases, where these are likely to have been caused or made worse by work, and a doctor confirms the diagnosis.

The health diseases specified in the Reporting of Injuries Diseases and Dangerous Occurrences Regulations (RIDDOR) (bit.ly/2rcQahC) Regulations 8 and 9 are:

- Carpal tunnel syndrome
- Cramp of the hand or forearm
- Occupational dermatitis
- Hand-Arm Vibration Syndrome
- Occupational asthma
- Tendonitis or tenosynovitis of the hand or forearm
- Any occupational cancer
- Any disease attributed to occupational exposure to a biological agent.

Industrial Injuries Disablement Benefit (IIDB) Scheme

If a worker has an industrial disease, advise them of the IIDB scheme, which provides financial support for some industrial conditions such as occupational asthma and carpal tunnel syndrome.

Further Advice and Resources

- ♦ See Chapter 36 on Equality and Disability
- ♦ Extensive guidance on the types of work which might cause these diseases are available at <u>HSE Guidance on RIDDOR</u> (bit.ly/2rc2Zsr)
- ♦ <u>The process of reporting diseases</u> (bit.ly/2sjTPe0) and a copy of the form (number F258a) is available on the HSE website
- ♦ <u>Industrial Injuries Disablement Benefit (IIDB) Scheme</u> (bit.ly/2vkwJaM) the UK Government overview on how to apply and the benefits available.

8. Vibration

8.1 Hand and Arm

Regular and frequent exposure to vibration can lead to a disabling condition called hand-arm vibration syndrome (HAVS) and carpal tunnel syndrome (CTS), caused by operating hand-held power tools (such as road breakers), hand-guided equipment (such as compactors), or by holding materials being processed by machines (such as pedestal grinders).

Damage occurs from long-term vibration affecting the tiny blood vessels, nerves and muscles of the hand and fingers. Occasional exposure is unlikely to cause ill health. The severity of the HAVS increases with more usage of hand-held tools and is an irreversible process. The most commonly seen health issue is <u>vibration white finger</u> (bit.ly/2sltnDT), which leads to severe pain and disability in the affected fingers.

Identifying the signs and symptoms at an early stage is crucial to preventing serious long-term health effects, which, if they occur due to work, is reportable as an occupational disease under RIDDOR (see Chapter 7.)

The early signs of HAVS are tingling and numbness in the fingers and loss of strength/grip in the hands. In the cold and wet, the tips of the fingers go white, then red, and are very painful when they warm up again.

HAV's can be prevented, but once the damage is done, it is permanent and can have an impact on normal daily activities (e.g. picking up small objects, working in cold weather).

A few simple measures can prevent the onset of HAVS:

- ♦ Use the right tools for the job and avoid gripping or forcing a tool
- ♦ Good circulation is key to preventing HAVS so keep hands warm and dry
- ♦ Stop or cut down on smoking as it reduces blood flow in the fingers

The first step is to assess how much vibration is occurring; use a hygienist (see Chapter 33) to measure the vibration levels or contact the equipment manufacturer for information. Businesses can also buy tools that measure vibration.

The amount of time a worker uses the equipment is the primary indicator of whether vibrations injuries occur and there is a chart available as a free download on the HSE website: Vibration Calculator (bit.ly/2pYqB6y)

Health Checks for HAVS

It is essential that workers report early signs of HAVS so that an investigation can take place. Due to the risks associated with the prolonged use of vibrating equipment, health checks are 'tiered' based on exposure years and symptoms:

Tier 1 (initial stage):	**New workers must complete a medical questionnaire prior to using vibrating tools.**
Tier 2:	**An annual medical questionnaire to be completed by those working with vibration. <u>Annual HAVs Questionnaire</u> (bit.ly/2038V6T). If health problems noted in either stage 1 or 2, workers move to the next tier up.**
Tier 3:	**This medical assessment is supervised by a qualified person (e.g. occupational health nurse with specialist training in HAVS assessments), done every three years irrespective of whether a person has shown any symptoms or not.**
Tier 4:	**Carried out by an occupational health doctor who also has a specialist qualification in HAVS assessments.**
Tier 5:	**An optional referral for specialist tests to confirm a suspected diagnosis of HAVS and find out if it is work-related.**

As a rule, workers should have health surveillance if using hand-held powered work equipment, and are:

♦ Likely to be regularly exposed above the exposure action value of 2.5m/s² A(8);
♦ Likely to be occasionally exposed above the action value and where the risk assessment identifies that there may be a risk to health;
♦ Known to have a diagnosis of HAVS, even if exposure is below the action value.

8.2 Whole Body Vibration

Heavy plant machinery and riding over uneven stony ground causes back pain from the constant vibrations transmitted up through the seat of the vehicle or machine. Whole body vibration is defined as shaking or jolting of the human body through a supporting surface (usually the seat or floor). For example, when driving or riding on a vehicle on an unmade road, operating earth-moving machinery or standing on a structure attached to powerful, fixed machines which are impacting on the ground or vibrating.

In drivers, back pain is worsened by:

♦ Having poor design of controls, making it difficult for the driver to operate the machine or to see properly without twisting or stretching
♦ Not adjusting the seat position for each person correctly, so having to continually turn, bend, lean and reach to operate the machine
♦ Sitting for long periods without changing position
♦ Having a poor posture
♦ Repeated manual handling and lifting of loads by the driver
♦ Excessive exposure to whole-body vibration, particularly to shocks and jolts
♦ Repeated climbing into or jumping down from a high cab or one difficult to get in and out of.

The risk increases where the driver or operator is exposed to two or more of these factors together.

There are specified limits to the amount of vibration over a working day of:

♦ 1.15m/s2 A(8)- exposure limit value – must not be exceeded
♦ 0.5 m/s2 A(8) – exposure action value – employer must take action to reduce risk

There is no prescribed health check for whole body vibration, but the risk assessment process should identify the risks and controls needed to minimise problems and the HSE suggests a symptom monitoring programme by a suitably trained person.

Further Advice and Resources

♦ HAVS information for workers (bit.ly/2pYUXG2)
♦ Carpal Tunnel Syndrome (bit.ly/2qL8oql) Information from the NHS
♦ Hand-Arm Vibration at Work from the HSE (bit.ly/2qKJYNF)
♦ Control of Vibration at Work Regulations 2005 (bit.ly/2pYobou), the specific law to protect against vibration injuries aimed at protecting workers from risks to health from vibration.
♦ Guidance on the regulations from the HSE vibration web pages (bit.ly/2pXPOOB) including all the questionnaires for workers
♦ Vibration calculator and guidance (bit.ly/2sl4bxn) from the HSE
♦ Six Ways to Measure Vibration (bit.ly/2yLPlTA)
♦ For further information: Control Back Pain Risks from Whole Body Vibration (bit.ly/2qE9Lby)
♦ See Chapter 36 on Equality and Disability

9. Manual Handling

Construction has one the highest rates of musculo-skeletal disorders (MSD's) such as bad backs, neck and shoulder injury etc., due to the physical nature of the job. Symptoms may include pain, aching, discomfort, numbness, tingling and swelling.

Activities that cause MSDs

Construction has one of the highest rates of MSDs. The most significant cause of injury is manual handling, which includes lifting, lowering, pushing, pulling and carrying. However, handling heavy objects is not the only cause of damage - MSDs can also result from doing a task repetitively, even if the load is relatively light (e.g., bricklaying), or where the person's body position is awkward or cramped (e.g. tying rebar).

Other everyday construction tasks associated with MSDs include:

- ◆ Block laying
- ◆ Handling pipework
- ◆ Laying kerbs and paving slabs
- ◆ Moving and installing plasterboard
- ◆ Installing mechanical and electrical equipment at height

The manual handling risk assessment and training should focus on controlling risks, rather than learning how to lift heavy weights.

Prevention of Injury

It may not be possible to prevent all incidents of injury due to manual handling, but there are things you can do, at work, to help prevent symptoms occurring or getting worse.

Health monitoring is an informal, non-statutory method of surveying your workforce for symptoms of ill health, including lower back pain. This enables you to be aware of health problems early and intervene. Another role of health monitoring is to feedback into a system that reviews the current control methods.

In addition, there are specific regulations dealing with manual handling in the workplace. To ensure you are complying with your duties under the law you should refer to HSE guidance if manual handling is a risk in your workplace.

How to carry out health monitoring

- ♦ Consider the method and frequency of monitoring when planning and implementing control measures
- ♦ Encourage workers to report health problems early. Have a brief, simple questionnaire for affected workers to fill in
- ♦ A body map can help a person to pinpoint where they are feeling the symptoms, and they can be asked to describe the sensations they are feeling
- ♦ Ask employees whether their work caused the problem and whether they can identify what specific task caused the pain.

If workers report symptoms, consider a referral to an occupational health provider, a physiotherapist or suggest they see their GP to get treatment. Many businesses have on-site facilities for these.

Reviewing

Reviewing the results of your health monitoring provides an opportunity to look at the overall performance of control systems and identify susceptible individuals.

You may have access to occupational health (OH), their advice is invaluable for managing that individual.

MSD problems can be specific to an individual, and each person is different and will need to be dealt with on a case-by-case basis, so you may need to consider:

♦ If a task is causing or contributing to an MSD, the worker may need to stop doing that part of the job for a time; temporarily modifying their duties could assist with recovery
♦ Return to work plans agreed by all parties and actively reviewed. If the individual has been off work, it is possible to return before all the symptoms have cleared up totally, provided that there isn't contrary medical advice
♦ Putting systems in place to help workers to return to work

If an MSD is recognised and treated early, workers usually recover fully.

Further Advice and Resources

♦ MSD's webpage (bit.ly/2xFu6RT) from the HSE
♦ The Back Book (bit.ly/2xGgB4l) by Kim Burton et al
♦ Guidance on the Manual Handling Regulations (bit.ly/2ftrFLM)
♦ Risk assessment of pushing and pulling (bit.ly/2xGJwW7)
♦ Body mapping: Telling where it hurts (bit.ly/2furIa1) USdaw Union leaflet
♦ See Chapter 36 on Equality and Disability

10. Noise

Over 1 million employees in the UK are exposed to levels of noise that puts their hearing at risk, with claims for hearing loss continuing to rise across all industries.

There are a number of ways to know if there is a problem on your site:

- ◆ Long-term employees may not hear conversations or warning shouts
- ◆ Reports from your medical service suggesting further hearing tests are required at the hospital or employees being referred to their GP
- ◆ Employees complaining of ringing/permanent background noise in their ears (tinnitus (bit.ly/2ftRvPL))
- ◆ Workers adapting their work to account for their poor hearing (for example, won't use the telephone, have instructions written down)

High-risk workers (sometimes termed 'safety critical') such as plant operators and scaffolders are usually required to have a reasonable level of hearing, that is, able to hear alarms and shouts for help , due to the nature of the work and the potential for injury and harm.

Health Checks

For those working in noise hazard areas, start with a pre-placement and then regular hearing tests A health record will be required under the Control of Noise at Work Regulations (bit.ly/2rGcyQJ) for workers regularly exposed to noise over 85 dB(A). Employers should undertake regular noise monitoring of work areas to ensure noise levels are controlled.

Other workers may be eligible for hearing tests if the noise levels are sufficient and the individual particularly sensitive to noise.

The medical check should also include health information for the worker and reasons for wearing hearing protection.

Ways to help employees who already have hearing loss:

- Make sure ear protection is available, so the remaining hearing is protected
- Make sure the employee is safe in emergency situations and hears warning bells; you may need to adapt the workplace, e.g., flashing lights instead of alarm and a buddy system to help in fire evacuations
- Recheck noise risk assessments
- Provide specially designed headgear/PPE to allow the wearing of a hearing aid

Return to work

Hearing loss occurs slowly over time, so workers may not be aware they have a problem. Reduced hearing can also occur after an accident to the head or some types of tumours.

It may be necessary to move the employee to other work on a temporary or permanent basis.

Further Advice and Resources

- The HSE Noise Web pages (bit.ly/2rG3M4W) sets out the daily and weekly limits for noise levels plus free guidance
- See Chapter 36 on Equality and Disability

11. Skin

Working with a physical, chemical, or biological agent or a repeating force can cause permanent skin diseases such as dermatitis (some call it eczema) and forms 80% of all work-related skin diseases.

There are different types of substances that can harm the skin – some irritate, and others cause permanent damage.

On construction sites, the primary skin hazard is cement dust mixed with sand or other substances to make mortar or concrete. Cement dust released during bag dumping or concrete cutting can also irritate the skin. Moisture from sweat or wet clothing reacts with the cement dust to form a caustic solution. Some workers may become allergic to the dust, with symptoms ranging from a mild rash to severe skin ulcers.

In addition to skin reactions, components of the dust can cause a respiratory allergy called occupational asthma (bit.ly/2yOCvnd). Symptoms include wheezing and difficulty breathing.

It's possible to work with cement for years without any problems and then suddenly develop an allergy. If the worker continues with an allergy then it is likely to worsen until exposure to even minute quantities triggers a severe response. An allergy such as this, usually lasts a lifetime and prevents any future work with wet concrete or powder cement.

When a skin condition first appears, the worker can apply creams to the affected area or avoid the substance altogether, but if exposure continues, a more severe skin condition of allergic dermatitis occurs. Here, large areas of skin become inflamed from just tiny exposures and the worker has to avoid altogether, which, if you are a bricklayer or plasterer, is hard to do.

Eye contact

Exposure to airborne dust may cause immediate or delayed irritation of the eyes. Depending on the level of exposure, effects may range from redness to chemical burns and blindness.

Assess the risk

A risk assessment needs to establish known substances that can cause skin allergy and identify measures required to protect all workers.

Look at safety data sheets for phrases such as:

- R42 or 43: May cause sensitisation by skin contact
- Skin sensitiser
- S24

Identify where concrete is used and see if you can reduce the amount used or even if it is necessary. Minimise the likelihood of direct contact with concrete and educate workers, so they know how dangerous it is to have concrete slurry remain on your skin.

Concrete burns

The hazards of wet cement are due to its caustic, abrasive, and drying properties. Continuous contact between skin and wet concrete allows alkaline compounds to penetrate and burn the skin.

Wet concrete or mortar can also fall inside a worker's boots or gloves; the result may be first, second, or third-degree burns or skin ulcers. These injuries can take several months to heal and may involve hospitalisation and skin grafts.

Make sure your first aiders know what to do when concrete accidents occur and call them for their opinion in cases of accidents.

Avoid skin burns:

♦ Wear the right PPE for any task involving wet concrete
♦ Gloves should be waterproof and suitable for use with high alkaline substances. They should be extended and/or tight fitting at the end to prevent cement being trapped between the glove and the skin
♦ Provide footwear such as wellington boots with no leaks or splits
♦ Wear waterproof trousers over boots and not tucked in
♦ Coveralls with long sleeves and full-length trousers (pull sleeves down over gloves and tuck pants inside boots and tape at the top to keep mortar and concrete out)
♦ Use knee pads or a waterproof mat for kneeling
♦ Provide washing facilities to wash off concrete quickly

Work practices

♦ When laying concrete block, have different sizes on hand to avoid cutting or hammering to make them fit
♦ Work in ways that minimize the amount of cement dust released
♦ Where possible, wet-cut rather than dry-cut masonry products
♦ Mix dry cement in well-ventilated areas
♦ Make sure to work upwind from dust sources
♦ Where possible, use ready-mixed concrete instead of mixing on site
♦ When kneeling on fresh concrete, use a dry board or waterproof kneepads to protect knees from water that can soak through fabric
♦ Remove jewellery such as rings and watches because wet cement can collect under them

Hygiene

♦ Quickly remove clothing contaminated by any cement - wet or dry. Wash affected skin immediately with large amounts of cold, clean water.

- Don't wash hands with water from buckets used for cleaning tools.
- Provide adequate hygiene facilities for workers to wash hands and face at the end of a job and before eating, drinking, smoking, or using the toilet. Facilities for cleaning boots and changing clothes should also be available.

Health Checks

Under the COSHH regulations, health surveillance may be required for this work, especially if it is difficult to control the risks or you are only relying on PPE to protect workers.

The most common type of health check is a visual inspection by someone trained to look for such problems (occupational health services or responsible persons) on a regular basis. Health questionnaires that ask workers to self-report possible skin problems, in my experience, are not reliable. Workers either hide their health problems, fearing their jobs may be at risk or just tick all the boxes.

Dermatitis, when diagnosed by a doctor is a reportable disease under RIDDOR (see Chapter 7)

Advice for Workers on Typical Treatments

Steroids

Steroid creams or ointments are commonly used to relieve scaling and extreme itching. Topical corticosteroid creams and lotions are available with or without a prescription but may cause harmful side effects if not applied correctly. Talk to your local pharmacy or GP before using.

Antibiotics

Antibiotics are only available from a GP and used to treat bacterial infections, open sores, or cracking in the skin caused by frequent scratching.

Antihistamines

Antihistamine tablets stop severe itching. Certain types might make you sleepy, helping not only to eliminate itching but also helping anyone whose sleep is affected by the urge to scratch. Be aware that these may affect driving or if you are in control of heavy plant on construction sites.

Oral or Injected Corticosteroids

Doctors prescribe steroid injection for extreme cases of itching. Although this treatment is effective for dermatitis, it is a short-term solution due to potential side effects.

Patch Testing

Patch testing identifies the causes of dermatitis. Here, doctors place patches of possible irritants on the skin to look for allergic reactions. Remember to test your own workplace suspects, such as cement dust and epoxy resins used on your site. I always include small samples for the worker to take to the patch testing appointment.

RAST Testing

Another option to help find the cause of dermatitis is through RAST (radioallergosorbent) Testing (bit.ly/2yOvXET); a blood test, which determines environmental and food allergies that can be contributing to skin sensitivity.

Further Advice and Resources

- ◆ Case Study: Healthy Skin in Construction (ubm.io/2fvk5Af) from SHP Online
- ◆ Skin at Work (bit.ly/2fx9Dbf) HSE website
- ◆ Construction Hazardous Substances: Cement (bit.ly/2fuXt2z) HSE
- ◆ Allergic Dermatitis (bit.ly/2gM2IeY) - general information from Wikipedia
- ◆ See Chapter 36 on Equality and Disability

12. Construction Dust

Construction dust is a broad term used to describe different dusts on a construction site; it is more than a nuisance - it can kill. Regularly breathing dust over a long time causes life-changing, debilitating lung diseases.

There are three main types:

♦ Silica dust – created when working on silica-containing materials like concrete, mortar and sandstone (also known as respirable crystalline silica or RCS)
♦ Wood dust – when working on soft and hardwood, plus other products such as MDF and plywood
♦ Less dangerous dusts – created while working generally, the most common, include plasterboard, limestone, marble and dolomite.

Diseases from breathing in these dust include:

♦ Lung cancer (http://bit.ly/2vvS6WI)
♦ Silicosis (bit.ly/2rErCBk)
♦ Chronic obstructive pulmonary disease (bit.ly/2cciMm1) (COPD)
♦ Work-related asthma (bit.ly/2vvNCzi)

Further Advice and Resources

♦ To see the full information sheet on working with dust and control methods, download the free information sheet Construction Dust (bit.ly/2rEn0vi) from the HSE
♦ See Chapter 36 on Equality and Disability

13. Contaminated Land

The UK has many chemical contaminants in soil, caused by industrial and domestic pollution in the past. Land contamination can pose a threat to the environment and the health of humans, animals and plants with:

- Heavy metals, such as arsenic, cadmium and lead
- Oils and tars
- Chemical substances and preparations, like solvents
- Gases
- Asbestos
- Radioactive materials

Most soil contains small amounts of contaminants, but generally, levels of risk are usually low. However, ex-industrial and landfill sites may pose an unacceptable level of risk to human health and may need remedial treatment before building work begins.

Further Advice and Resources

- Technical and health information available from DEFRA[3] (bit.ly/2s2j3QY)
- Overview of contaminated land (bit.ly/2voeXD0) from Gov.UK
- Land Remediation and Waste Management Guidelines (bit.ly/2gWhNKZ) from Scottish Environment Protection Agency

---

[3] Department for Environment, Food and Rural Affairs (formerly MAFF)

14. Confined Space Working

A confined space has two defining features:

1. The workplace is substantially enclosed.
2. There is a reasonably foreseeable risk of serious injury from hazardous substances or conditions within the space or nearby.

Some confined spaces are easy to identify (e.g., closed tanks, vessels and sewers). Others are less obvious, but may be equally dangerous (e.g., open-top tanks or constructions that become a confined space during their manufacture).

Health Issues

Some workers may be more at risk from working in confined spaces than others, such as:

♦   Have a health issue such claustrophobia, asthma, diabetes.
♦   Have difficulty wearing breathing apparatus
♦   May find it difficult to escape in emergency situations due to physical conditions (breathing problems, obesity, gripping)

If there is a reasonably foreseeable risk of serious injury in entering and working in a confined space, a 'permit to work system' (bit.ly/2ttZtdf) may be required; a formal method statement of safe steps to take and authorised by a qualified person in the business before work can start.

What Health Problems to Look for

Necessary precautions and issues to consider:

- The nature of the confined space, e.g., trench or tank
- Hazards, such as lack of oxygen, chemicals, fumes or vapours
- Contamination from adjacent plant or processes
- Increased fire risk
- The type of work, e.g., welding would increase the risk of fire, and noisy environments would make communication difficult and/or affect long-term hearing
- Emergency response (e.g., first aid availability, evacuation)

Confined Space Principles

The first priority on any site is to avoid confined space working as much as possible. If unavoidable, then a competent person must develop the system of working in it. In complex or high-risk situations, specialist assessors may have to do the assessment.

Medical Considerations

There is no statutory requirement for workers to have a medical test; it makes sense to:

- Consider the suitability/fitness of individuals who will be working in a confined space as well as available rescue and resuscitation equipment (e.g., harnesses, oxygen, etc.)
- Arrange health checks (such as a safety critical medical) to test for fitness to work in a confined space (e.g., able to escape, hear and see adequately)

Further Advice and Resources

- Working in Confined Spaces (bit.ly/2tzcjHd) the HSE website
- Safety-critical workers' health checks (bit.ly/2tz0ykc) video

15. Working in Heat

Heat stress can occur when working in compressed air in underground tunnels and dams. Seasonal changes in the outside air temperature can be a significant contributor to heat stress.

Heat stress occurs when the body's means of controlling body heat starts to fail. As well as air temperature, factors such as work rate, humidity and clothing worn while working may lead to heat stress.

Monitor the health of those at risk of heat stress carefully. If there are a large number of workers involved, engage a health professional to oversee the risk assessment process and control measures.

Further Advice and Resources

♦ For more information go to the <u>heat and heat stress section on the HSE website</u> (bit.ly/2t3sgpM)

16. Office Work

The Health and Safety (Display Screen Equipment) Regulations (bit.ly/2rjtMTP), sets out how to deal with computers, workstations and, more recently, mobile technology to prevent ill health amongst users.

I hear all sorts of pains and ailments people think are due to using display screen equipment - issues such as headaches, neck pain, skin rashes, poor eyesight. Many of these problems would go if everyone applied some simple rules, as set out below.

How to Set Up Workstation

The most effective way of preventing health issues is in educating users on how to set up their own computer workstation. Occupational health and safety practitioners should promote training in the use of IT equipment and be part of the induction programme so that myths and poor practice are nipped in the bud

Display screen assessments are different, depending on your company; but nothing beats a proper old-fashioned evaluation done by an 'expert', that is, those adequately trained in how to do it.

The Top 10 Errors of DSE

I have done many DSE assessments and here are my top 10 errors which I find:

1. Chair set up incorrectly for comfort
2. Not using the equipment correctly, e.g., keyboards, mouse, mats
3. No training on software programmes
4. Layout of equipment not efficient, especially if left-handed
5. Not taking regular work breaks from intensive keyboard work
6. Poor housekeeping, limiting movements of chair and body by storing boxes under the desk or cluttering the desk
7. Reflections on the screen
8. Using bifocal or varifocal spectacles (causing neck pain)
9. No footrest, creating pressure on the back of the legs
10. Sitting too long at the desk with no exercise or changes in position

Follow the excellent guidance as set out in the further resources section below for the best ergonomic set up of equipment and workspace.

New Equipment

It is helpful to apply the general principles of the DSE regulations to any new requests for equipment – does the chair comply with DSE regulations? If not then a new one may be required. However, an 'all singing and dancing' chair is part of the law and once one person in a shared office has one then, in my experience, they all want one! So be aware of the implications of recommendations and under what rules you allocate new equipment. No one is impressed if, after buying a £1000 chair, you find the same health issues arise three months down the line because the user doesn't adjust it correctly.

In cases of disability, specialist equipment may be required. See Access to Work (Chapter 35) for information about disability and equipment.

Many health conditions related to computer work are usually cleared by paying attention to the first set-up, especially posture, chair adjustment training and taking regular work breaks. However, there will be health issues, which may need a further investigation.

Some health issues linked to computer use, such as carpal tunnel are reportable to the Health and Safety Executive (HSE) under RIDDOR (see Chapter 7)

Physiotherapy can help in most cases. Occasionally short-term restrictions from working at a computer can help, but total rest from display screen equipment work is only needed when the there is a severe problem.

See also Chapter 17 for information on eyesight testing and how to set this up.

Working from Home

Many workers are opting to work from home now. Users carry laptops back and forth from work, logging in to local networks, and sit at communal hot desks. Very rarely have I seen any of these workstations fully and correctly adjusted to suit the worker, even though the equipment is fully adjustable.

At home, users sit at the dining room table on a stool or even balancing a laptop on their laps and seem willing to tolerate this in exchange for the 'working from home' benefits. However, it should be emphasised that home workstations have the same requirements in law as the office; assessments and equipment should have equal importance.

Remember to review DSE assessments when there are significant changes in the setup. This can include software programmes, new equipment, office moves and organisational change resulting in new work patterns.

Pads, Tablets and Laptops, Visual Display Units (Dashboards)

Nowadays tablets, pads and visual display units are an integral part of work life. Dashboards should be ergonomically assessed for ease of use and have the ability to show a dangerous situation or warnings easily.

Health issues occur from texting, inputting and working in cramped conditions; such as texting thumb, or shoulder and neck pain from prolonged use of tablets in unusual surroundings. Holding the tablet for extended periods can cause finger and wrist problems too.

Laptops are portable computers not designed for long periods of work. However, an appropriately set up workstation, with separate screens and keyboard quickly adapt a laptop to a healthier alternative.

Due to their portable nature, a range of hazards need addressing when considering the safe use of both tablets and laptops:

- Ergonomic issues such as body posture, frequency and length of sessions, and method of use
- Manual handling issues relating to transport and handling
- Electrical hazards
- Noise
- Trip hazards associated with the electrical cord
- Personal security issues

Maintaining proper body posture is difficult when using a tablet, pad or laptop as users compact their shoulders and necks to see and use the screens for extended periods, increasing the risk of injury.

Tablets and Laptops

Many use tablets in awkward postures such as sitting or lying prone on the floor. Despite its name, a laptop is not designed for long-term work on your lap. Also using a tablet horizontally can cause problems. Avoid these positions for long-term work. Also be aware of reflections on screen causing difficulties with posture and concentration.

General Tips for Mobile Devices

- Where tablet/laptop usage exceeds 30 minutes of continual work, take short rest breaks of 5 minutes for every 30 minutes of work, and use stretching techniques to ease muscle soreness
- Take note of the lighting and reflections, making sure sun glare does not cause visual disturbance
- Enlarge the print or change the contrast or brightness for better viewing
- Maintain a comfortable viewing distance from the screen
- Tilt the screen of the laptop so that it is angled like the pages of book for easy reading
- Wherever possible, use suitable computer aids such as docks, laptop stand/cradle, an external keyboard, an external monitor, an external mouse, documents holders
- Cables should not be a trip hazard
- Keep earphone audio levels to a minimum to prevent excessive noise exposure
- Keep elbows close to the body whilst operating portable devices
- Keep your head and neck in a relaxed posture and avoid excessive neck flexion or rotation
- Turn off mobile devices when not in use
- Check electrical input and tagging of the electrical cords
- Use a suitable carry-case or bag when transporting
- Consider how you carry equipment. Do you need to take it with you and if so, is it balanced (use a backpack and not a briefcase)
- It's easy to spot a laptop case or backpack; so beware of thieves
- Do not use equipment when driving or walking - many construction sites have banned the use of mobile phones when out on site due to safety concerns

Record Keeping

Keep copies of completed display screen equipment assessments in a user's file and in a place that is easy to check.

Further Advice and Resources

- HSE website for DSE (bit.ly/2rjq8sO)
- Vision and Work (bit.ly/2rjyy3z) - Blog
- DSE and how to set up correctly (bit.ly/2rjCxx7)
- Blog: Buying DSE Equipment- (bit.ly/2rjuws5)
- A DSE assessment form is available on my website (bit.ly/2qVDPy2) registration required
- How to ergonomically set up your laptop as a desktop (article) (bit.ly/2xGZwHz)
- The assessment form can be developed in-house or from the HSE Guidance on Regulations 'Work with Display Screen Equipment' (bit.ly/2rjq8sO)
- See Chapter 36 on Equality and Disability

17. Vision

Vision is one of the critical senses used for protecting ourselves, but sadly, it deteriorates over time.

Driving

In order to drive cars (Class 1) to the biggest lorries (Class 2) – vision is essential for road and site safety.

The official current eyesight requirements for driving on UK roads is updated and published on the Gov.UK website (bit.ly/2sPTccx).

All drivers must be able to read a number plate from a certain distance (with glasses if necessary), and there are rules about having sight in only one eye etc.

Lorry drivers have to have a full eyesight test as part of their medical test for the licence, called a D4 examination (bit.ly/2sMxPIV).

There is no specific legislation on the vision of plant operators unless they drive on public roads. However, most set out their own company standards and these usually follow the requirements as set out for Class 2 drivers or the Constructing Better Health ((bit.ly/2tQv7Sg) standard for vision.

Computer (DSE) Users

Under the Display Screen Equipment Regulations, (bit.ly/2rjtMTP) employers have to offer an eyesight test to those who are classified as a DSE user, and this can be done via your own occupational health service or optometrist.

In order to cut down on double testing, I always recommend full examination by an optometrist using a voucher or via a local provider because a complete test serves two purposes – full compliance with the Regulations, plus extra tests for glaucoma (bit.ly/2oshabI)

Occupational Health Vision Testing/Screening

Vision is usually measured on-site measured using the <u>Snellen</u> scale (bit.ly/2s9iAfZ), the big letters on a white card that you read with one hand over each eye, or an automated machine such <u>as a</u> <u>Keystone</u> (bit.ly/1m8tT9m) or <u>OPTEC</u> (bit.ly/2yLBdcG) vision screener.

Corporate Schemes for Vision Testing

Formerly, I used the voucher systems for eyesight testing for DSE, safety specs and drivers but there were problems with the vouchers expiring (they have about a 3-month shelf life). We would buy books of the coupons and find that half of them had expired.

My answer was to go to one of the biggest supermarket chains (Tesco) who run their own service. They offer online access to vouchers which never expire, friends and family discounts, points on purchases, parking and have outlets in most towns plus an automated invoicing system based on what you had used across the UK (and they were cheaper). The only downside that I discovered was that there were not many optician outlets in an area of Scotland where we had many drivers, but there is a map which shows where your nearest store with an optician is – just put your postcode in the provided map.

Further Advice and Resources

- ◆ Corporate schemes for eyesight testing
  - ▪ <u>Tesco</u> (bit.ly/2sX3cAr)
  - ▪ <u>Specsavers</u> (bit.ly/2sXmyFG)
  - ▪ <u>Vision Express</u> (bit.ly/2sXhUYj)
- ◆ For issues with vision affecting driving, check on the government driving website <u>A–Z list of health conditions</u> (bit.ly/2s8JDrQ)
- ◆ See also the <u>RNIB website</u> (bit.ly/2sd1Ww0) regarding sight loss.

Colour Vision

People with colour vision problems find it difficult to distinguish between different colours, often called 'colour blindness'. Colour vision deficiency can vary in severity. People with colour vision deficiency may have difficulty identifying pale colours or deep colours if the lighting is poor. Others will experience a very slight difference in the way they appreciate different hues and shades of colour. In rare cases, a person may experience many colours that all seem the same.

There are two main types of colour vision deficiency, either red-green or blue-yellow.

Most people know they have a colour vision problem if they cannot name colours correctly. However, in mild cases, colour deficiencies may go undetected.

Later on in life, it could affect the type of employment choice that a person may make, for example, an electrician may have difficulty distinguishing specific wire colours, which is potentially dangerous.

I do not think that traffic light signals are an issue even though green and red are opposites (stop and go). The placing of the lights makes it easy to see which light is on and which is not; but for jobs, such as pilots and air traffic controllers, accurate colour recognition is imperative.

Colour Vision Tests

There are several tests for checking colour vision. In an occupational health (bit.ly/2FOwKph) setting, the Ishihara test (bit.ly/19DTEaI) is usually the test of choice.

Practical Working Tests

In the workplace, an operational assessment is necessary if a job depends on distinguishing specific colours – for example, a work test using coloured objects to see if you can pick the correct object or make a decision based on shades of colour.

For work where colour vision is essential to health and safety, employers tend to adapt the workplace or even take out the part of the job that includes the need to distinguish between colours, but sometimes that is not practical.

Further Advice and Resources

- More information on who can have a free <u>eyesight test in the NHS</u> (bit.ly/1bLgV1U)
- <u>Colour vision deficiency (colour blindness)</u> (bit.ly/2xIe5La)

18. Safety Critical Work (SCW)

Vehicles and equipment operate which work on construction sites, such as specialised lifting gear, cranes, lift trucks, heavy goods vehicles, dumpers, or plant - are significantly more dangerous than on the public highway, due to the terrain, lack of clear roadways and purpose of vehicles.

Due to this, the employer/PC needs take into account the individual employee's fitness both in respect of activities where an employee's fitness may be likely to affect personal health and safety and where it may affect others.

Analysis of fatal injuries to workers in all industry show that construction industry is the leading cause of death in 2016/17 figures:

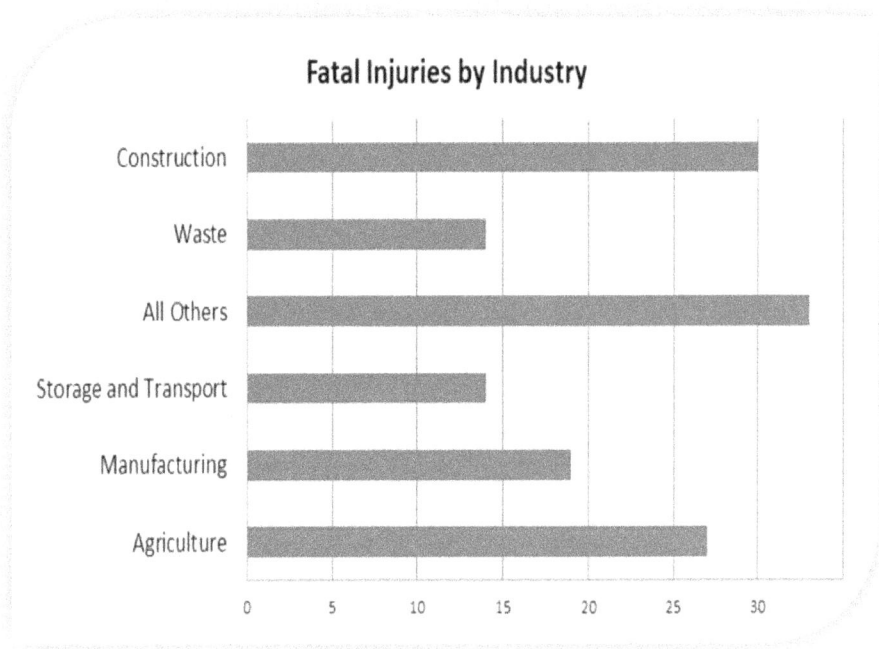

Fatal Injuries by Industry

Industry	Value
Construction	30
Waste	14
All Others	32
Storage and Transport	14
Manufacturing	19
Agriculture	27

And although this is a safety issue; health has a huge impact on workers and their ability to work safely.

Here, courtesy of the HSE, are the main kinds of accidents happening across all industries in the UK for 2016/7.

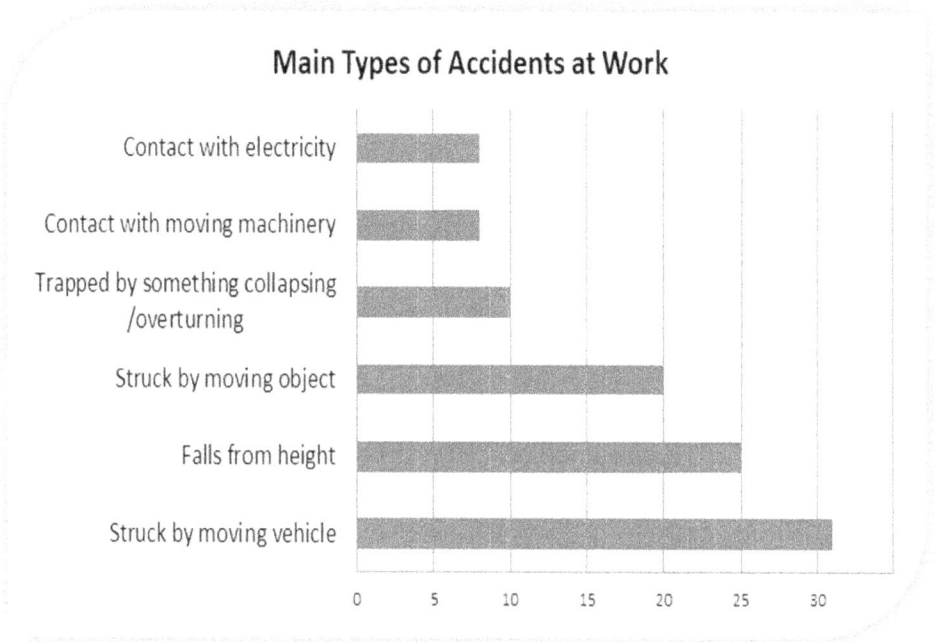

Main Types of Accidents at Work

Type of accident	Value
Contact with electricity	~7
Contact with moving machinery	~7.5
Trapped by something collapsing /overturning	~10
Struck by moving object	~20
Falls from height	~25
Struck by moving vehicle	~31

What is a Safety Critical Worker?

The risk assessment that identifies an activity as 'safety critical' in the construction industry distinguishes between:

1. The risk of harm to the individual worker
2. The risk to other workers and third parties

As a rule, workers should not work in high-risk situations if there is a risk of:

♦ Sudden loss of consciousness
♦ Impairment of awareness or concentration

- Sudden incapacity
- Impairment of balance or coordination
- Significant limitation of mobility

It is best practice to undertake a medical enquiry prior to allowing workers to begin working in these high risk areas although it is a legal requirement.

The Medical Examination

Usually, a health professional does the medical assessment that takes about 30 minutes and includes:

- A general health questionnaire
- Blood pressure test
- Hearing test/breathing test(optional)
- Testing mobility of head, neck, limbs
- Vision test
- A urine sample to check for diabetes
- General health discussions (e.g., days off sick, visits to GP)
- A drug and alcohol test is optional depending on company policy
- Drivers must report any health issues immediately to their supervisor and be reminded about the effects of drugs and alcohol on their driving capabilities.

Frequency of Medical Checks

- Plant operators need medicals before training starts and at regular intervals after; although frequency varies from annually to every five years
- Many regimes for medicals increase in frequency as the worker gets older due to loss of physical capability, e.g., Class 2 drivers
- Repeat health check after a work accident or long-term absence

Failing a Medical

In my experience, the two most common reasons for "failing" safety critical or high risk medical is high blood pressure or poor eyesight, both of which are quickly dealt with by the GP or optician.

Drivers who have a health condition that affects driving should be temporarily suspended from operating plant and site driving until the health condition has either been treated successfully or resolved.

Occasionally a permanent health problem occurs, when a driver cannot safely return to his or her job; in these cases, redeployment or dismissal are the only options available (see Equality Act below).

Further Advice and Resources

♦ What a <u>safety critical medical in construction involves</u> (bit.ly/2qW6R0w) video
♦ The Strategic Forum Plant Safety Group has produced <u>Medical Fitness for Plant Machinery</u> (bit.ly/2pBU1Hg) available as a free download and includes information on all aspects of health and fitness plus advice on disability and recruitment.
♦ HSE guidance <u>Rider Operated Lift Trucks</u> ACOP L117 (bit.ly/2t3rBEB)
♦ Equality Act and implications are available from the <u>Government Equalities office</u> (bit.ly/2rd212t)
♦ <u>Constructing Better Health</u> (bit.ly/2tQv7Sg) are discussing taking out the term 'safety critical' for construction workers in their documentation, although I imagine it will take some time for SCW to be entirely removed from our vocabulary

19. Drivers

Figures suggest that up to one-third of all road traffic accidents involve somebody who is at work at the time; and accounts for over 20 fatalities and 250 serious injuries every week.

When are accidents most likely?

- On long journeys on monotonous roads, such as motorways
- Between 2am and 6am
- Between 2pm and 4pm (especially after eating, or an alcoholic drink)
- After having less sleep than normal
- If taking medicines that cause drowsiness
- After long working hours or on journeys home after long shifts, especially night shifts

Medical Standards for Drivers

The Driver and Vehicle and Licensing Agency (DVLA) sets out clear medical standards for all drivers both Class 1 (Cars) and Class 2.

There is no law to say that a medical check is required for Class 1 licences, but there are strict procedures for Group 2 licences (for example, heavy goods vehicle or minibus), reflecting the larger size and weight of these vehicles and the increased time the driver is likely to spend at the wheel.

Some medical conditions, such as epilepsy and diabetes, require regular reviews by the DVLA for a specific period, and there is a requirement for drivers to inform the DVLA of health problems that could affect their driving.

Drivers on public highways must tell DVLA if:

- They develop a 'notifiable' medical condition or disability

- ♦ A medical condition or disability has worsened
- ♦ Notifiable conditions include:
  - ▪ Epilepsy
  - ▪ Strokes
  - ▪ Nerve and mental health conditions
  - ▪ Physical disabilities
  - ▪ Vision problems

DVLA controls driving issues on public highways with advice about licences, driving categories, medical conditions and reporting health issues.

The full list of health conditions and situations (bit.ly/2tWEnVe) and when you need to inform the DVLA

On-Site Driving

As many construction sites are not on the public highway, so technically the DVLA rules do not apply, in which case the employing organisation sets the standards for driving on their own property.

Larger construction companies often employ occupational health (OH) services (*see Chapter 28*) to provide additional non-statutory health checks such as annual health checks or vision tests.

An OH service can do both statutory and non-statutory medicals or could review drivers who may be experiencing difficulties with driving duties or after an illness or long-term sickness. Although, in my opinion, statutory health checks for Class 2 drivers, best sits with the workers own GP who has access to all the past medical history, rather than just the work history.

There are many factors which affect driving:

- Alertness and related factors (e.g., tiredness, alcohol, drugs)
- The driver's mood and other activities taking place in the vehicle (e.g., carrying additional passengers, using mobile phones, eating and drinking)
- How experienced a driver is and their risk-taking behaviour
- The age of the driver, for example, younger drivers tend to have better eyesight than say, someone over fifty years old.

Any of the above issues could have an impact on site safety and should be considered in the risk assessment for preventing road and site accidents.

Further Advice and Resources

- The Highway Code (bit.ly/2sMRqIM)
- Department of Transport information (bit.ly/2sMOz2H) about driving at work and road safety
- Having a medical examination to drive a bus or lorry (D4 category) from DVLA? Download the free guide (bit.ly/2sMxPIV)
- Health promotion for healthy truckers (bit.ly/2sXfF7m) Blog
- See Chapter 36 on Equality and Disability

20. Working at Height

Did you know that falls from height accounted for a quarter of fatal injuries across all industries 2016/17? The majority of falls are from ladders and vehicles.

Dangers of working at height are well known, and there are many instances of work at height in construction:

- Crane drivers
- Scaffolders
- Roof workers
- Aerial riggers, e.g., high aerials, telephone/radio masts, power pylons
- Deep level workers may be required to climb steep vertical ladders, often within confined spaces

The climb to and from the work area must be safe and climbers able to both deal with the difficult nature of the work and able to maintain safety, e.g. ability to grip, balance.

Each task requires a full risk assessment and includes hazards in the environment such as high wind and a comprehensive rescue plan in case of medical emergency.

Work at Height Health Checks

Occupational health service providers often do health checks prior to working at height, consisting of:

- A general health questionnaire
- Blood pressure test
- Hearing or whisper test/breathing or lung function test(optional)
- Testing for coordination and mobility of head, neck, limbs, etc., also a weight check
- Vision test
- A urine sample to check for diabetes as a minimum

- ♦ General health discussions (e.g., days off sick, visits to GP)
- ♦ A drug and alcohol test is optional depending on company policy(see Chapter 22 for more information)

Further Advice and Resources

- ♦ <u>Work at Height Regulations 2005</u> (bit.ly/2t0ai7j)
- ♦ See Chapter 36 on Equality and Disability

21. Fatigue

Fatigue is a state of physical and/or mental exhaustion that reduces a person's ability to perform work safely and efficiently. Fatigue reduces alertness, leading to errors, and an increase in workplace incidents and injuries.

Fatigue was a contributory factor to some of the most significant disasters of our time: the Three Mile Island accident in Pennsylvania, the Chernobyl nuclear power plant accident in Russia, and the grounding of the oil tanker Exxon Valdez off the coast of Alaska. Also, 20% of accidents on major roads, have fatigue as a sole or contributory cause, and costs the UK £115 - £240 million per year in terms of work accidents alone.

Causes of Disturbed Sleep or Fatigue

Problem	Notes
Insomnia	Difficulty falling asleep, or cannot stay asleep for a full night. By waking during the night, too early, not able to fall asleep at night, or have difficulty getting back to sleep if awakened. Insomnia can be either short term, in response to a stressful event or change in environment, or long-term.
Sleep apnoea	Excessive daytime sleepiness is a tendency to fall asleep at inappropriate times while intending to stay awake and comes under the heading of a sleep disorder. The most well-known is obstructive sleep apnoea (bit.ly/2r9RGAT) in 4% of men. But 28% in lorry drivers. The symptoms include loud habitual snoring and sudden gasping for air - observed by others. Formal diagnosis and treatment require referral to a specialist sleep clinic (bit.ly/2r6sEm8).

Narcolepsy	Sudden sleep "attacks" where a person will have an uncontrollable urge to sleep many times in one day.
Substances	Nicotine, caffeine, and alcohol affect the quality of sleep. Alcohol may shorten the time to fall asleep, but disrupts sleep later in the night. Nicotine also disrupts sleep and reduces total sleep time. Over-the-counter medications or prescriptions may also affect rest.
Diabetes	Some need insulin injections on a strict timetable through the day and night
Heart and Circulatory	Affects physical stamina levels
Stomach and Intestinal	The time you eat is essential for keeping some health conditions controlled
Chest/breathing problems	Symptoms may interfere with sleep
Medication Timetable	Medical conditions requiring medication on a strict timetable, shift work may interrupt the programme
Treatments	Cancer treatments can affect fatigue levels
Ageing	Between 40 and 45 years of age, changes occur in the internal biological clock which affects the quality of sleep, causing sleep to become easily disrupted, particularly on night shifts
Interrupted sleep	New mother, fathers, environment, housing issues, worries
Long-term conditions	For example, multiple sclerosis, Motor Neurone Disease, Parkinson's, Seasonal Affective Disorder
Mental Health	Work events can be emotionally tiring and increase fatigue. Home problems also cause distress and lead to fatigue, e.g. bereavement or personal conflicts.

Pregnancy	Frequent trips to the toilet, uncomfortable positioning and increasing girth may disrupt sleep
Jet Lag	Symptoms of excessive sleepiness and a lack of daytime alertness for those travelling across time zones
Shift Work Sleep Disorder	This sleep disorder affects people who frequently rotate shifts or work at night.

Fatigue increases with:

♦ Dim lighting
♦ Limited vision (i.e., due to fog, cloudy day, rain)
♦ High temperatures
♦ Loud noise
♦ Being very comfortable
♦ Tasks sustained for long periods of time
♦ Work tasks which are long, repetitive, paced, challenging, tedious or monotonous

Workplaces can help by providing environments that have good lighting, comfortable temperatures, and reasonable noise levels. Work tasks should offer a variety of interest and tasks should change throughout the shift.

If extended hours/overtime is standard, consider the time required to commute home, meal preparation, eating, socialising with family, etc.

Workplaces may wish to consider providing:

♦ On-site accommodation
♦ Prepared meals for workers
♦ Facilities for taking a nap before they drive home

If fatigue and sleepiness persist, workers are advised to see their doctor or an occupational health service if available.

Workplace Fatigue Policy

Develop a fatigue policy for all workers, managers and supervisors, which should include:

- Maximum shift length and average weekly hours
- Work-related travel including flying to and from different time zones
- Procedures for reporting fatigue risks and managing tired workers.

Reducing Fatigue at Work

- Minimise permanent nights
- Minimise sequence of nights, only 2-4 night shifts in succession
- Consider shorter night shifts
- Avoid quick change-overs
- Plan rotas with some free weekends
- Avoid overlong work sequences
- Rotate forward (i.e., clockwise rotation morning/ evenings/ nights)
- Avoid early starts
- Limit periods of excessive mental or physical demands, e.g., through job rotation
- Ensure fit for purpose plant, machinery and equipment
- Make sure workloads are manageable. Take into account workflow changes due to factors such as machinery breakdowns, unplanned absences or resignations. Avoid unrealistic deadlines.
- Where possible, be aware of personal circumstances that affect workers and provide support.

Scheduling

Try to schedule tasks evenly throughout a shift. A person's ability to be alert or focus attention is not constant throughout the day. For most people, low points occur between 3.00am and 5.00am, and between 3.00pm and 5.00pm. During these low-function times, adopt a conservative approach to safety and avoid high-risk tasks such as:

- Working at height
- Heavy manual handling demands
- Confined space working
- Operating mobile plant

Further Advice and Resources

- Healthy Work: Managing stress and fatigue in the workplace (bit.ly/2r9zPu0)
- The HSE's 'fatigue risk index' for shift workers (bit.ly/2r9FBvq)
- Reducing error and influencing behaviour: Health and Safety Guidance (bit.ly/2r9G40E) HSG 48
- Case Study on Tunnellers: Crossrail and Fatigue, factsheet and legacy project (bit.ly/2r9zA29)
- Stopmakeachange resources (bit.ly/2r9CZxG) pages includes many tools on tiredness and fatigue

22. Night Work

Night work is a specific hazard identified by law in the <u>Working Time Regulations</u> (bit.ly/2r6lEWF) as having the potential to harm health, yet many night workers thrive on night work and have done so for years without any ill health effects. Around 3.6 million people report to working shifts 'most of the time'. Shift work has its advantages for both employers and workers, from maximising plant use and reducing production costs, to better earnings for fewer hours' work and opportunities for flexitime.

Night work is defined as working at least three hours at night (on a regular basis), between the period of 11 pm and 6 am. Employees who do the occasional night (rather than routine night work) do not fall into the category of night worker.

Night Work and Health

The regulations set out that all night workers should be offered a health assessment before starting night work, followed by health assessment at regular intervals; this is generally repeated annually (although not specified in the regulations).

The health assessment takes the form of a health questionnaire completed by the employee, followed, if necessary, by a health check. The questionnaire will identify medical conditions that could pose a potential risk to health and safety.

A medical is offered on a voluntary basis. There is no legal obligation on the employee to complete a questionnaire or attend a medical check because of night work.

What is a Night Workers Health Assessment?

The Health and Safety Executive (HSE) has identified undesirable consequences to working nights, including:

- Disruption of the body clock
- Fatigue
- Sleeping difficulties
- Disturbed appetite and digestion
- Reliance on sedatives or stimulants
- Social and domestic problems

Although the HSE is responsible for enforcing compliance with health assessments for night work, there is no specific guidance on what this entails.

Strategies range from a comprehensive set of health checks such as blood pressure, cholesterol, height/weight advice and urine sampling, whilst others have only offered a telephone consultation.

This is what I do and recommend for night workers:

- Ask the night worker to fill in a general health questionnaire and send it to me in a sealed confidential envelope
- I check the questionnaire for health issues I believe may be affected by night work
- If the worker wants a health check; I make an appointment to see them and discuss their personal health (that may be affected by night work)
- Usually I check their height, weight and blood pressure and give relevant health advice depending on the person
- I have only once suggested a worker is not able to do night work and that was due to pregnancy related health issues.

Further Advice and Resources

- ♦ The <u>Working Time (Amendment) Regulations</u> (bit.ly/2r6lEWF)
- ♦ The effect of <u>pregnancy on night work</u> (bit.ly/2r6dWMg) from the Royal College of Physicians.
- ♦ See <u>Shift Work and Guidance</u> (bit.ly/2r6C3u9o)
- ♦ For general guidance on working hours, including health assessments go to the <u>ACAS website</u> (bit.ly/2r6t4Jg)
- ♦ <u>Night worker health check questionnaire</u> to be administered by health professionals only (bit.ly/2xybx23) from Working Well Solutions
- ♦ See Chapter 36 on Equality and Disability

23. Drugs and Alcohol

Both drugs and alcohol (D & A) affect concentration and physical coordination of workers, which can lead to dangerous behaviours. This is relevant when considering the safety-critical nature of specific jobs on and around construction sites and the potential for catastrophic events.

The possession of some drugs is illegal; whilst some prescribed and over-the-counter medicines have side effects that severely affect safety.

Alcohol too can affect productivity, performance and team morale leading to bad behaviour and poor discipline.

If employers make a policy decision to treat alcohol or drug problems as a health issue, it is much more likely that workers will ask for help; rather than trying to hide their addiction and possibly cause accidents etc.

Definition:

The definition of drug and alcohol misuse is:

- ◆ Alcohol dependence, excessive consumption and inebriation in the workplace
- ◆ Taking or possessing illegal drugs
- ◆ Misusing legal substances such as prescribed medicines
- ◆ The misappropriation of solvents, e.g., inhalation of gases or glues

Drug and Alcohol Policy

A drug and alcohol policy ranges from a general statement regarding the problem to a comprehensive document outlining full drug and alcohol testing on a regular basis.

Testing for drug and alcohol has been mandatory in the railway industry for some years, and many construction companies have adopted that procedure; already testing for both D&A to ensure that workers are safe to work on sites and to protect members of the public from accidents due to misuse.

If you want to do the same, think carefully about what screening to do and what you do with the information you receive. Consider the testing process itself, including the type of testing, how the sample is collected and the security of the sample from contamination.

D&A problems seem to be increasing and so too does the requirement for drug and alcohol policies and, in some cases, even testing. Many large construction companies have a D&A policy in the contract of employment, yet sub-contractors and the self-employed (who visit the site) may not. Despite this, when a sub-contractor is on a construction site, they will fall under the terms of the principal contractor policy and testing regime.

Businesses should encourage users to come forward, in the first instance, and offer support for those affected, rather than punish them. However, you must make it clear that possession or dealing in drugs at work will be reported to the police.

Legal Position for Drug and Alcohol Management

There are general and specific laws that employers use to justify an action for drug and alcohol offences, e.g. The Health & Safety at Work etc. Act (bit.ly/2tpcFQA) and Construction (Design and Management) Regulations (CDM) (bit.ly/2vixKgx)

Usually, the principal contractor prepares, develops and implements a written plan and site rules for health and safety; the relevant parts are shared with contractors for overall site compliance. The site drug and alcohol policy would be such a document to share and for compliance.

Procedure for Drug and Alcohol Testing

Drug and alcohol testing is legally fraught, so it's essential to follow strict guidelines if considering doing testing. Start with

86

your own company policy and, if you are a subcontractor ask to see and understand the policy on any sites you visit – these rules will probably overrule your own.

Every construction company should have their own D&A policy available for workers and subcontractors to see, prior to starting work on site.

Common drugs to test for include

- ♦ Amphetamines
- ♦ MDMA (ecstasy)
- ♦ Benzodiazepine
- ♦ Cannabinoids (THC)
- ♦ Opiates including heroin, morphine
- ♦ Cocaine
- ♦ Methadone
- ♦ Propoxyphene

Results are usually reported as a PASS or FAIL by the testing authority.

Also:

Legal Highs

'Legal Highs' produce the same or similar effects, to drugs such as cocaine and ecstasy, but not controlled under the Misuse of Drugs Act. They are, however, considered illegal under current medicines legislation to sell, supply or advertise for "human consumption."

There are a large number of 'legal highs', and they can have all kinds of names, including brand names and chemical names, for example, Dimethocaine, Benzo Fury, 5IAI, MDAT, Silver Bullet, and Ivory Wave.

Gases, Aerosols and Glues

Solvents cover a vast number of substances: gas lighter refills, aerosols containing hairspray, deodorants and air fresheners, tins or tubes of glue, some paints, thinners and correcting fluids, cleaning fluids, surgical spirit, dry-cleaning fluids and petroleum products. When inhaled, solvents have a similar effect to alcohol. They make people feel uninhibited, euphoric and dizzy.

Slang: Thinners

Drug Testing Process

You can either train your own staff to do drug and alcohol testing or contract a specialist service. Whichever service you choose, the final test must be from an accredited laboratory.

These can also provide:

- Information on how to develop a drug and alcohol policy
- Guidance on the methods of drug testing (e.g., urine, breath, hair, saliva) and the implications of each process
- Information about the resources that might be needed for the workplace (e.g., chain of custody, customising toilets, testing equipment, cost of testing)
- Advice on when to undertake drug and/or alcohol tests (e.g., pre-placement testing, random testing, 'for cause' testing after incidents and to demonstrate compliance with rehabilitation programmes)
- Guidance on referral routes for employees who admit to having a problem (e.g., local services, Alcoholics Anonymous).

What's the Impact on Your Workers?

Testing of workers for drugs and alcohol is a serious step, and not straightforward. The test results are affected by:

- When the last drink was taken
- The effects of different drugs on specific individuals
- The fact that some drugs cannot be tested for
- Medications such as ibuprofen that can interfere with test results
- The availability of testers when there is an incident
- Whether you do a dipstick (instant) type test for drugs or send a sample to the laboratory for full testing (can take from 24 hours to five days)

It is good practice to offer help and support to workers who have a drug or alcohol problem. This ensures the employer retains a valuable worker and aware of any potential safety issues. However, once a test has proved the presence of drugs or alcohol, the worker is usually subject to disciplinary action - that is, workers cannot claim dependency and ask for help after testing - only before.

Further Advice and Resources

- A sample D&A policy available on Working Well Solutions (bit.ly/2skrreW) site registration is required
- Advice from the European Workplace Drug Testing Society (bit.ly/2x1INhE) on reliable and accurate drug testing processes
- "Talk to Frank" website (bit.ly/2x1a8AX) full of information on all sorts of drugs and substances and their effects: click here
- The NHS drug dependency (bit.ly/2x1u729)
- The NHS alcohol misuse and addiction (bit.ly/2x1sfq4)
- Find the nearest drug addiction support service (bit.ly/2xoQ3KK)
- HSE information about drugs and alcohol at work (bit.ly/2xoZFFu)
- Alcoholics Anonymous (bit.ly/2x1nvku)
- Guidance from the Trades Union Congress on drug and alcohol (bit.ly/2x1a9EO)

24. Personal Protective Equipment

Personal protective equipment (PPE) protects the user against health or safety risks at work. It can include items such as safety helmets, gloves, eye protection, high-visibility clothing, safety footwear, and harnesses. It also includes respiratory protective equipment (RPE).

Consider

♦ The risk involved and the correct type of protection (e.g., the fabric of gloves may increase the risk of harm by absorbing chemicals rather than repelling them)
♦ Individual differences, e.g., men and women, tall and short
♦ The correct selection of the various kinds of PPE available for the hazard (e.g., using a dust mask for fumes, means the mask does not stop the fumes, the smaller molecules pass straight through the filter and inhaled by the worker. Workers, believing they are protected could work longer in the fumes, and closer to them, in the mistaken belief that they are protected)
♦ Manufacturers who may be able to offer specific/specialist advice

Also

♦ Adopt PPE only after on-site risk assessment process and all other means of reducing risk have been explored using the hierarchy of control
♦ Carry out employee health checks as part of an ongoing health surveillance program to check the adequacy of your control methods, which includes the use of PPE

Face Fit Testing

Respiratory protection equipment (RPE) such as face masks and respirators, must fit the face. Otherwise, leaks occur. The problem is that workers with leaky masks are likely to be more at risk because they may be totally relying on the protection.

As people come in all shapes and sizes, it is unlikely that all RPE is going to fit every size and shape of the face to stop leaks adequately, which is why face fit testing is required.

RPE fit testing must be done by a competent person; there are specialist courses available. The British Safety Federation (bit.ly/2u2D0CV) has more information to help you decide and/or chose a tester.

Things to consider:

- ♦ How tight the mask has to be? Is it comfortable?
- ♦ Different jobs and the amount of RPE needed (each user will need to have face fit testing)
- ♦ Facial hair may interfere with a good seal

The type of PPE required will depend on the hazards involved and the part of the body needing protection (see Table).

Types of PPE

Protect	Hazard Examples	Options
Eyes	Chemical or metal splash, dust, projectiles, gas vapour, radiation	Safety specs, googles, face shields, visors
Head	Falling or flying objects, bumps, hair entanglement	Helmet or bump caps
Lungs	Dust, vapour, gases, fume, oxygen deficient atmospheres, toxic chemicals	Masks, respirator, air fed helmets, breathing apparatus
Body	Extreme temperatures, weather conditions, chemical or metal splash, spray, impact or penetration, dust and entanglement of clothing	Overalls, boiler suits, specialist clothing
Hands & Arms	Abrasion, temperature extremes, cuts and puncture injuries, impact, chemicals, electric shock, skin infections, disease and contamination	Gloves, gauntlets, mitts, wrist cuffs
Feet & Legs	Wet, static charge, slipping, cuts and puncture injuries, falling objects, metal and chemical, abrasions	Safety boots, shoes with protective toecaps, gaiters, leggings, spats.

More employer duties:

- Cannot charge employees or agency workers for PPE
- Must replace PPE if it is worn or damaged
- Must ensure that workers are given training on the need for PPE and its correct use
- Workers won't wear PPE willingly if it is not comfortable or if it interferes with the job, so it's important to consider this before buying. Suppliers of PPE are usually happy to let you sample products before purchasing.

PPE must be:

- Adequately assessed to make sure it is suitable for the users and the substance
- Maintained and stored properly
- Supplied with instructions on how to use it safely
- Marked with the CE marking (a manufacturer's declaration that the product complies with the essential requirements of the relevant European health, safety and environmental protection legislation)

Further Advice and Resources

- The HSE offers resources and guidance (bit.ly/2qIebgh) on The Personal Protective Equipment at Work Regulations
- Guidance on PPE (bit.ly/2qIebgh) from the HSE
- Respiratory Protective Equipment at Work (bit.ly/2u2Giay), a practical guide HSG53 from the HSE
- Face-fit testing guidance from the HSE (bit.ly/2qIffjX)

25. Work-Related Cancers

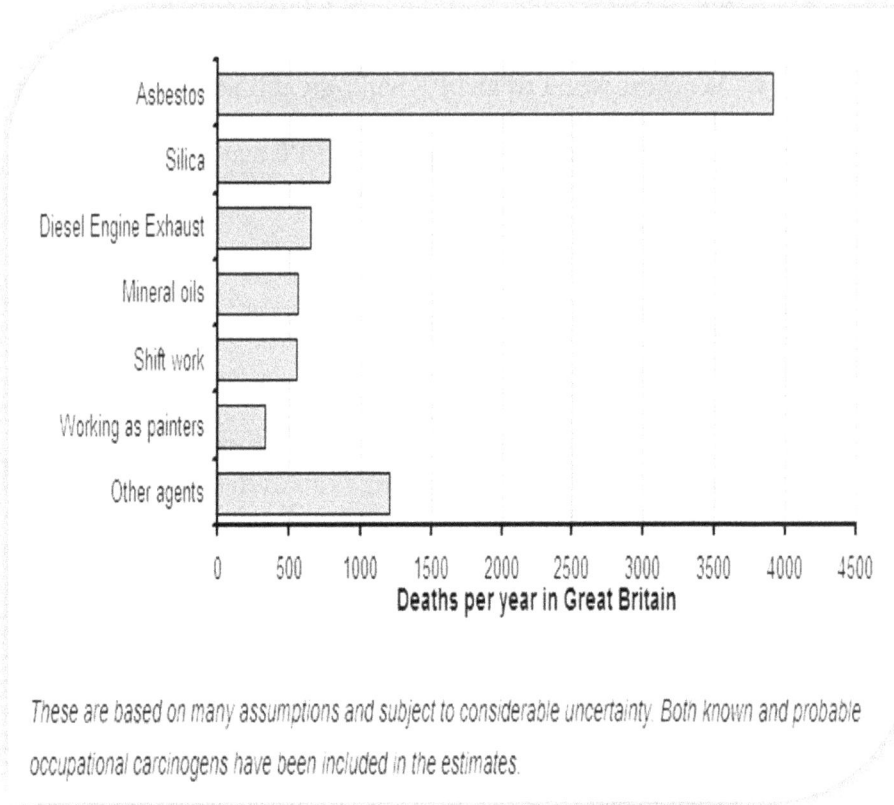

Asbestos	
Silica	
Diesel Engine Exhaust	
Mineral oils	
Shift work	
Working as painters	
Other agents	

Deaths per year in Great Britain

These are based on many assumptions and subject to considerable uncertainty. Both known and probable occupational carcinogens have been included in the estimates.

HSE chart above showing estimated job-related cancers in GB 2005

Did you know the construction industry has the largest estimate of occupational cancer cases, with 3,500 cancer deaths and 5,500 cancer registrations each year? The leading cause of deaths, being asbestos exposure which continues today.

Exposure to silica, diesel engine exhaust, solar radiation, shift work and working as painters and welders might become the leading causes of occupational cancer in the future, according to the HSE research study (bit.ly/2vvU8WK); whereas deaths from asbestos are likely to lessen due to restricted use now.

What Else Affects Cancer

Work may not be the only issue when considering the development of cancer. It's important to remember the influence of other factors; such as age, smoking, alcohol and genetics. Estimates suggest that 85 percent of lung cancers are linked to smoking, making it by far the most significant cause of cancer.

Equality and Disability

The Equality Act automatically covers workers with cancers; in which case, employers have to make reasonable adjustments to the workplace and keep an employee at work or return to work after illness.

Included in this section are the following cancers, which have been identified by the HSE as the leading causes of cancer in construction:

1. Skin cancer
2. Silica
3. Diesel engine exhaust
4. Painters

25.1 Skin Cancer

Spotting the Signs of Skin Cancer

Incidence rates for melanoma skin cancer are projected to rise by 7% in the UK between 2014 and 2035, to 32 cases per 100,000 people by 2035.

- ◆ The numbers of malignant melanomas in the UK has quadrupled in the past 30 years
- ◆ The highest occupational group to get skin cancer is in construction

- Over a third of malignant melanoma cases occur in people under 55
- The most common site to develop skin cancer for men is on the chest or back; for women, it is on the legs. But other places can be affected too, such as the sole of the foot or face
- Sun exposure is the primary cause of skin cancer although sun bed use produces the same effect

Remember though that exposure to the sun has a number of benefits – it makes you feel good, helps the body to create vitamin D and provides opportunities to undertake physical activity.

Advice for Workers

- Wear a hat
- Use a sunscreen with a sun protection factor of 15 or more
- Keep shirts on in sunny weather
- Avoid working in the sun at and around midday
- As part of health promotion, workers should regularly check their skin for unusual spots or moles that change size, shape or colour

Workers should check their skin regularly and remember the ABCD rule when checking moles:

- Asymmetry – the two halves of the mole may look different
- Border – edges of melanoma may be irregular, blurred or jagged
- Colour – the colour of the melanoma may be uneven with more than one shade
- Diameter – many melanomas are at least 6mm in diameter, the size of a pencil eraser

It is important to note that moles are just one sign of skin cancer and there are others. Also, changes in the skin may not be due to skin cancer. In both cases, you should always check out anything suspicious on your skin with your own Doctor.

25.2 Silica (Respirable Crystalline Silica)

Silica is a natural substance found in rocks, sand and clay and the dust breathed in when cutting bricks and concrete. Exposure can lead to silicosis, lung cancer. It can also cause the chronic obstructive pulmonary disease (COPD) (bit.ly/2r6m3bo) which is not cancer but it has been proposed as a carcinogen in Annexe 1 of the Carcinogen and Mutagen Directive (2004/37/EC). In the USA a limit has been issued for those working with RCS.

HSE estimates that around 500 deaths occur every year due to workplace exposures to RCS in Great Britain.

Advice for Workers

Always comply with your employers or site health and safety rules. If you have a cough for over three weeks - go see your doctor or occupational health services if you have one.

25.3 Diesel Engine Exhaust (DEE)

Breathing in diesel fumes over a short period can affect health, and exposure to the fumes can cause irritation of the eyes or respiratory tract.

Workers most at risk from cancer due to DEE in construction are those:

♦ Working with diesel operated heavy vehicles
♦ Working near motor vehicles such as when coming into and out of car parks or when passing toll booths
♦ Workers in tunnels
♦ Construction sites which use diesel operated stationary power sources (e.g., generators)

The quantity and composition of diesel fumes may vary depending on:

- ◆ Quality of diesel fuel used
- ◆ Engine type, e.g., standard, turbo or injection
- ◆ How tuned the engine is
- ◆ The fuel pump setting
- ◆ Workload demand on the engine
- ◆ Engine temperature
- ◆ Maintenance of the engine

Advice for Workers

Always comply with your employer's or site health and safety rules. If you have a cough for over three weeks - go see your doctor or occupational health services if you have one.

25.4 Painters

Painters in construction do many tasks, for example, sanding, filling, painting or spraying. This means coming into contact with the following hazardous substances:

- ◆ Solvents
- ◆ Lead
- ◆ Construction dust
- ◆ Asbestos
- ◆ Pigments, resins and catalysts

All of which can cause health problems in the long term.

Research suggests that the most common types of cancer for painters in construction occur in the lung, bladder and stomach although paint technology has improved with paints becoming water rather than solvent-based.

Advice for Workers

Always comply with your employer's or site health and safety rules. If you have a cough for over three weeks - go see your doctor or occupational health services if you have one.

Further Advice and Resources

- For a full list of cancer-causing agents caused by occupation go to the Cancer pages of IOSH (bit.ly/2vwsKbb).
- Control of Substances Hazardous to Health (COSHH) Regulations (bit.ly/2vBTtmL)
- COSHH Approved Code of Practice (bit.ly/2vBR1N9)
- For more advice on how to manage diesel emissions (bit.ly/2ud2xuw), download the free leaflet from the HSE
- Cancer and Construction: Silica (bit.ly/2vBLt57) HSE mini website
- To see what a cancerous mole looks like go to NHS choices (bit.ly/2slfu92)
- The Cancer Research website (bit.ly/2t3vlpD)
- For more information and guidance on both solvents and paints go to Cancer and Construction: Painters (bit.ly/2vBTib0) from the HSE
- See also Construction Dust (Chapter 12)
- See Chapter 36 on Equality and Disability

26. First Aid at Work

First aid saves lives, prevent minor injuries from becoming more serious, and conditions getting worse before emergency services arrive. The Health and Safety (First Aid) Regulations (bit.ly/2t3p7X0) sets out the circumstances of why and how to provide first aid equipment, facilities and workers so that immediate assistance is available.

To decide the type of first aid arrangements, employers start by doing a first aid needs assessment. This considers factors such as:

♦ Numbers on site at all times (including contractors and visitors), especially during weekends and shift/night work
♦ Types of people at a location (e.g., inexperienced workers, workers with disabilities or those with health problems needing urgent help)
♦ Types of work, that is, the stage work is at - are you at ground investigation level or first fix? Requirements will change during the life of the project
♦ Distance from the local hospital and access routes for ambulances on site
♦ Characteristics of the site (e.g., size and layout of the site, location of workers)

The minimum necessary first aid provisions at any work site are:

♦ A first aid box
♦ A person to take charge of first aid arrangements
♦ Information about the first aid arrangements

Choosing Your First Aiders

Recruit suitable first aiders from the workforce. They should be:

♦ Discreet
♦ Trusted
♦ Calm in a crisis

- Able to pass the practical and written exam at the end of the course
- Interested in health matters
- Ready to be released from their own work in an emergency

Some companies offer extra pay for being a first aider.

First Responders

When working in high-risk environments such as tunnelling, many construction projects opt for a full-blown emergency response. For example, the Olympics had an accident and emergency centre that included on-site ambulances.

Providers of OH services can also be your emergency response team, providing treatment, primary care services and vaccination services. They can supervise and provide annual refresher courses with support for first aiders after serious incidents.

AED (Automated External Defibrillator)

With the increase in publicly available AEDs together with an employer's responsibility to ensure adequate first aid provision, I'm asked whether an AED should be made available at business premises.

There is no law in the UK to say businesses should provide an AED; but under English law, there can be a liability in negligence for failing to take appropriate safety precautions on your premises.

Remember if you decide to install AED's you will have to provide training, maintenance and instructions also.

Further Advice and Resources

- The Resuscitation Council (UK) and British Heart Foundation Guide to Automated External Defibrillators (AED) (bit.ly/2t3hFuX) full information about the use of AEDs and frequently asked questions.
- HSE information and resources on all aspects of first aid (bit.ly/2t3pAbL)
- First aid policy and risk assessment documents and guidance (bit.ly/2t3p7Xo) from Working Well Solutions

27. Mental Health

Mental health problems can affect anyone at any age, regardless of race, gender, or social background. Disorders range from mild anxiety to schizophrenia and change peoples' behaviours in different ways.

What Causes Stress in Construction

A recent survey identified the top five most stressful issues in construction as:

- Having too much work to do in the time available
- Travelling or commuting
- Being responsible for the safety of others at work
- Working long hours
- Having a dangerous job

The highest risk jobs are management, road maintenance staff, designers and administration staff, who report more stress than other job roles of labourers and operatives.

Statistics

- 1,400 construction workers committed suicide from 2011 – 2015
- Two-thirds of those were aged 40 and above, with those aged between 40 and 49 found to be at most at risk
- A Chartered Institute of Personnel and Development study4 has highlighted the impact on the business of poor mental health of employees. The study found that:
    - 37% of sufferers are more likely to get into conflict with colleagues
    - 57% find it harder to juggle multiple tasks

---

4 Acas.org.uk. (2017). <u>Mental health | Acas</u>. [online] May 2017

- 80% find it difficult to concentrate
- 62% take longer to do tasks
- 50% are potentially less patient with customers/clients.

♦ One in six workers experiences depression, anxiety or unmanageable stress, with the same number having sleep and fatigue problems

In response, many construction companies support new mental health initiatives such as:

♦ Mind Matters (bit.ly/2pKDeC4) from Construction News
♦ Mates in Mind (bit.ly/2pKsm7k) from Health in Construction and the British Safety Council
♦ Crossrail – focussing on mental health (bit.ly/2pKFsRX)

What to Do About Stress

Employers have duties to undertake a risk assessment for stress the same as other health and safety hazards. The primary law for stress is a general one, that is, Management of Health and Safety at Work Regulations (bit.ly/2qVrQAJ) and specifies the duty to do risk assessments, which would include a stress risk assessment.

For those undertaking safety critical work it is important to identify any serious mental health problem which has the potential to affect personal safety or that of others, for this reason it is important to assess mental health as part of the safety critical health check, although there is currently little in the way of verified ways of doing this. More advice is available in the Mental Health Toolkit (see below)

Further Advice and Resources

♦ Stress policy and risk assessment guidance (bit.ly/2uKQIih)
♦ For further information go to HSE website on stress (bit.ly/1HxYEUp)
♦ Mental Health Toolkit (bit.ly/2vDwuVl) for employers from Business in the Community

- Suicide Prevention Toolkit from Business in the Community
- For types of mental health problems and recommended treatments, go to the Mind website pages (bit.ly/2vE8Dou)
- Find an Employee Assistance Provider (bit.ly/2qpZpct) for talking therapies
- The Lighthouse Charity (bit.ly/2vDCQUS) provides a free telephone advisory service for all construction workers, telephone 0345 605 1956

Self help

1. Mood Zone (bit.ly/2pL6kkD) The NHS self-help website
2. GetSelfHelp at Get.gg (bit.ly/2pKQlmx)

From Working Well Solutions:

- Manager's Guide to Stress Risk Assessment (video): (bit.ly/2qVxh2i)
- Stress Prevention at Work advice from an international perspective (bit.ly/2qW39Eg)
- Go to my free templates download pages (you will have to register) for a simple stress policy and template guidance document on undertaking a conventional UK risk assessment (bit.ly/2qVDPy2)

28. Infections

Vaccinations protect workers from some diseases, and construction workers may be exposed to many, due to the nature of their work. Where potentially harmful diseases are involved, like tuberculosis, for example, it is essential to immunise workers and prevent an outbreak that could spread amongst others.

Employers and principal contractors must look at the potential risk from hazards such as contaminated soil, water, land or working in close proximity to animals

What Vaccination and Why

♦ Contaminated water and/or ground can pose a risk of infection from diseases such as <u>Weil's disease</u> (Leptospirosis) (bit.ly/2tp8HYk) and <u>Legionella</u> (bit.ly/2toPOop).
♦ Discarded syringes/hypodermic needles can accidentally pierce the skin causing viral infections such as <u>Hepatitis B</u> (bit.ly/2tp8Yuk) and <u>HIV</u> (bit.ly/2tp7nof)
♦ Other diseases such as psittacosis (parrot disease) and toxicaria (roundworms in dog excrement) may be transmitted from animals to humans.
♦ All workers exposed to metal/welding fumes should be given a single dose of the pneumococcal pneumonia vaccine
♦ Some business opt for the seasonal flu vaccination or pay for workers to have the vaccine locally (many pharmacies provide the service, e.g., Boots, Tesco, Sainsbury's)

Vaccinating workers for at-work risks is one solution but avoiding the risk altogether by other means is far safer.

Itinerant workers may not have access to health care so employers should make sure new employees are aware of any risk and have all the necessary vaccinations.

Sharp Injury Advice for Workers

Be aware that sharps may be present in the working environment

♦ Always wear the correct PPE; especially boots and gloves
♦ Be careful especially if you can't see what you are doing with your hands
♦ If you see a needle or broken glass tell your supervisor
♦ Quarantine any sharps and the area it was found in – there may be more you can't see

What should I do if I am injured by a needle?

♦ Do not panic; gently squeeze the area around the wound to encourage bleeding
♦ Do not suck the wound; clean the wound under running water, or use cleansing wipes provided in first aid kits
♦ Cover the wound with a dry plaster or dressing
♦ Keep the needle that caused the injury in a safe place; it may be needed by the doctor
♦ Contact with a needle can cause infection or spread disease so always seek medical advice and treatment immediately

Further Advice and Resources

♦ The Control of Substances Hazardous to Health Regulations (COSHH) (bit.ly/coshhregs) place duties on employers to minimise biological risk to workers' health.
♦ Guidance from the HSE (bit.ly/2tVdn8v) on the application of the COSHH regulations and other issues
♦ For more information regarding specific health issues, go the Health Protection Infectious Diseases webpages (bit.ly/2tp9mJf)
♦ The Green Book (bit.ly/2x4ezeh) has all the latest news on UK vaccination regimes, when and if required
♦ HSE Guidance on work infections (bit.ly/2toQIkL)
♦ Flu vaccination for welders (bit.ly/2fu891u)

29. Occupational Health (OH) Services

OH services, do any or all of the following health checks on workers:

- Pre-placement screening
- Safety-critical medicals
- Health and medical surveillance
- Attendance management
- Management referrals for health issues
- Drug and alcohol testing
- Well-being programmes
- Workplace assessments
- Health risk assessments

The Health and Safety Executive states that good occupational health services are central to the effective management of workplace health and can:

- Protect and promote the health and well-being of the working population
- Enhance a company's image and reputation as a good employer
- Provide early advice to help prevent workers being absent for health-related reasons
- Improve opportunities for people to recover from illness while at work
- Provide critical support to the process of effective absence management and increase the number of staff returning to work earlier
- Fulfil the statutory requirement to have access to 'competent' occupational health advice as part of the organisational arrangements to ensure that the health of staff and others are not adversely affected by their work

The starting point for deciding on how to monitor health is to assess the health risks in the workplace via the risk assessment process; this shows where there are significant residual risks to health remaining even after control measures are applied.

An OH service is a private medical service that an employer, client or principal contractor hires to look after the health of the workers. The OH service can be an in-house service, that is, employed directly or contractors. On the larger construction projects, there may be one or many OH services each advising the various subcontractors separately.

Which is better? Here are the pros and cons of having your own OH service.

Pros Of Having an Occupational Health Service

Of course, I would advocate an occupational health service. Otherwise, I would be doing myself out of a job, but let me look rationally at this question from an organisation's point of view. Here are the main issues to consider.

29.1 Legal

The overriding reason for companies to engage an occupational health service is to protect workers and for legal reasons. There are health and safety laws which says health checking is required, such as, the <u>Control of Substances Hazardous to Health Regulations</u> and the <u>Control of Noise at Work Regulations</u>. However, no law stipulates an OH service per se. So when would think about engaging one?

a. High-Risk Work

Work with high-risk compounds or processes such as asbestos, lead and compressed air can severely affect workers; so the law says workers must have statutory medical checks. These checks can be through an OH service or by other means such as a local doctor or an <u>HSE appointed Doctor</u>

b. Health Surveillance

If you use a substance or process where health checks might be needed (dependent on risk assessment), such as excessive noise, or chemicals, you may need an occupational health service. If you're not sure if this applies to you, visit the HSE website pages on health surveillance

c. Disability

Currently, the law says that anyone with a long-term health issue may fall under the Equality Act; in which case the employer has to make concessions. Although a health professional cannot make the concessions, they would be able to recommend if a worker is likely to be covered by the Act. For more advice about disability at work, read the Government guidance

29.2 Safety

Fitness for work is important too, not only for the worker but also for an organisation. For example, construction workers have to climb scaffolding or work with earth-moving equipment. These workers usually need a higher level of medical fitness than say somebody who works in an office. OH services offer these checks tailored to suit your workplace.

29.3 Absence

People fraudulently taking off time sick, is costly and disruptive for any organisation. Medical professionals challenge those who are regularly off sick and decide whether there is a valid reason or whether they are just playing the system. They report their findings back to the supervisor or manager in the form of recommendations. Once you have advice, you can either follow the advice or decide not to.

29.4 Wellbeing

You can start your own well-being programs tailored to your workforce; for example, if you have young males you might want to focus on identifying prostate cancers or if they tend to smoke, offer nicotine replacement. By raising awareness of general health issues and smoke-related lung diseases such as <u>COPD,</u> you may be able to influence their health behaviours, thus protecting their long-term health.

You may also incidentally improve their attendance.

29.5 Best practice

Purchasing your own OH service is an excellent strategy to enhance your image and retain staff. Your organisation could ease the burden on the local NHS service too.

Cons of Having an Occupational Health Service

Cost

a. Medical staff

Medical staff are expensive to hire because of their extended training and ability. Doctors are more costly than nurses, and nurses more expensive than technicians.

In-house medical staff need specialist insurance and continuing professional development and ongoing training, which is costly. Also, OH is a specialist qualification for both doctors and nurses, and there is a shortage in both areas, meaning that the cost is usually higher than other professional medical groups.

b. Time off work

You must allow time off work for workers to attend an OH appointments and reviews; maybe even referrals to specialists.

c. Equipment

Equipment here covers any cost of medical equipment such as lung function testing or perhaps an audio booth on site. Not only do you have to pay for the equipment if it's an in-house service but regular maintenance checks and peripherals as well. If you engage an external OH or visiting service, the cost is included in the contract, but in this case, there is the inconvenience of having to set up equipment each time, with problems of transport and clinic rooms to use.

Training

In order to have an efficient and effective OH service you want to train managers, HR, Trade Unions and employees on what they can and can't do through your OH service. Without the training, an OH service is often perceived as dysfunctional.

Policy/procedure

You will also need to write <u>policies and procedures</u> (bit.ly/2mGYuUH) for your company, covering the main points of referral, health surveillance and management actions.

Confidentiality

When employees talk to OH, the information they share comes under the umbrella of <u>medical in confidence</u>. Managers are then in the dark about the real reason for a person's absence. However, if you didn't have an OH health service, the employee would've probably shared everything with you, and you would have a full picture of what's going on. Some managers find the confidentiality aspects of an OH service to be obstructive to their management of a worker.

Time

Waiting for things to happen in OH sometimes takes a while. This is especially true when waiting for letters from GPs or specialist or perhaps trying to arrange appointments with reluctant employees.

You also have to add in how often OH services visit your site, time for reports to arrive, what to do when you receive a report and if you can carry out the changes. Without OH, a manager would do what s/he perceived as necessary. The manager is in control and acts when and how they want. Much simpler.

One way to control time-wasting is to set up a service level agreement with timeframes specified; such as:

'we will give an appointment to an employee within five working days of receiving the request'.

Click here for a simple example of a service level agreement (bit.ly/2zHHvtJ) from my website (you will have to register.)

But bear in mind that some things will be outside of the OH service's control, for example, the results from a drug and alcohol testing laboratory or specialist reports from an individual's NHS doctor.

Boundaries

You need to decide the type of service for your organisation; whether it's all singing all dancing, like a GP practice where your workers make appointments for themselves, or just the bare minimum service, to comply with the law. There are sometimes boundary issues between on-site departments such as HR and safety. Everyone needs to understand their roles, so there is no confusion. Responsibilities must be set out in both policy documents and during training programmes, to minimise potential problems.

Without boundaries for your service, workers and manager can become confused about the role of OH.

Loss of Control

Once OH is involved with a worker, the manager is relying on the recommendations to be workable and pragmatic. If they aren't then managers and OH professionals should confer. Without this last step, you will have raised expectations of the employee and wasted the referral process. Managers can be seen as obstructive too.

Evidence

It is worth bearing in mind that deteriorations in health over time will be evident in health records, and, a clear implication that the work has caused the loss of health. The health records, therefore, opens up the possibility of liability in law and used in evidence of lack of care on behalf of the employer, which workers can use for proof in compensation claims.

Experts

If you have an OH service and then ignore their recommendations or refuse to refer a worker to the service, you will be in a difficult situation if the case goes to court or arbitration. Once you have an OH service and policy and procedure, it is essential to consider their recommendations seriously, before rejecting what them. You can, however, argue that the recommendations did not meet your organisational needs.

So, have you made a decision? Which points are essential to your organisation?

The pro's and con's mentioned here, do not apply to all organisations, some industries are riskier than others. Also, there may be other factors to consider, such as size, place, spread and manager competence; plus the risk to the workers and the control measures already in place.

Occupational Health or GP

Or why not use a local GP. After all the GP is part of the NHS and knows the individual thoroughly?

GP's may know the individual, but they are also their advocate and must maintain a positive relationship with their patient. Most GP's do not understand the full implications of health and safety law, nor the responsibilities that an organisation has to its employees and the public at large.

Also, a GP advises an individual without specific knowledge of their job or health risks, whereas an OH service knows the law, the organisation, how it works and what is available for job adjustments.

List of OH Work

OH specialists will:

- Advise on work-related illnesses and accidents
- Carry out medicals on new starters and existing employees for fitness to work
- Monitor the health of employees who work in processes or with substances that could damage their health (e.g., hearing test for those who work in noisy areas)
- Assist with absence management.
- Protect the employer, employee and the company
- Train workers on preventing health risks
- Advise on ergonomic issues and workplace design
- Promote good health education programmes

To understand the various levels of medical and office support you need for medical matters go to the HSE website on competent advisers (bit.ly/1JWa1HS) to see the explanation of each level of services from the responsible person.

Do I need a Medical or OH Service for my Business?

Maybe it makes sense to engage your own OH service? Consider the flowchart below to clarify what is best for your organisation. Start with questions 1 - 3 to identify your priorities, with number one being the most important to number three being less so:

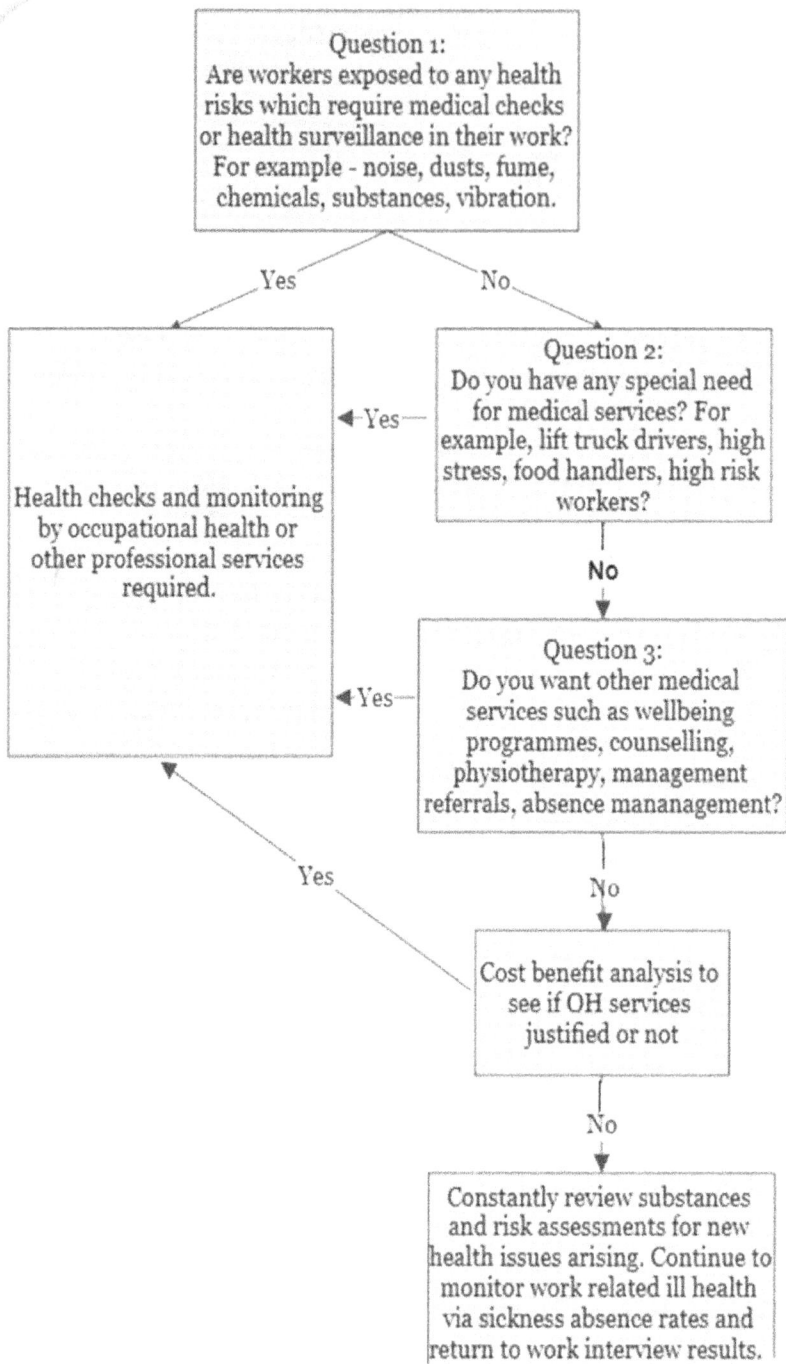

Question 1:
Are workers exposed to any health risks which require medical checks or health surveillance in their work? For example - noise, dusts, fume, chemicals, substances, vibration.

Yes → No →

Question 2:
Do you have any special need for medical services? For example, lift truck drivers, high stress, food handlers, high risk workers?

←Yes

No ↓

Health checks and monitoring by occupational health or other professional services required.

Question 3:
Do you want other medical services such as wellbeing programmes, counselling, physiotherapy, management referrals, absence mananagement?

←Yes

No ↓

Yes

Cost benefit analysis to see if OH services justified or not

No ↓

Constantly review substances and risk assessments for new health issues arising. Continue to monitor work related ill health via sickness absence rates and return to work interview results.

National helplines:

Still, don't know? If you don't have access to a medical service, consider using one of the national OH services, each has knowledge bases and a free helpline:

England and Wales:

- ◆ Fit for Work (bit.ly/2vBKFdH)
- ◆ 0800 032 6235

Welsh Language Line:

- ◆ Ffit I Weithio (bit.ly/2vBNbk7)
- ◆ 0800 032 6233

Scotland:

- ◆ Fit for Work Scotland (bit.ly/2vBzfGT)
- ◆ 0800 019 2211

Note the numbers - they are national helplines to help if you have a problem in the future or are unsure.

Types of Service

There are three different ways of having access to OH services in construction:

Client Provided:

The client pays directly for a shared occupational health facility for the whole construction workforce irrespective of the employer. The advantage is consistency. The disadvantage being cost. An example is the Olympic Delivery Authority.

PC Provided:

The PC sets up an OH service on each site/project, allowing subcontractors and supply chains employees to use the services with regular auditing of compliance.

Separate Services:

Each contractor and self-employed worker use or have access to their own OH schemes, that is, covering direct/employees only. Difficulties occur with monitoring OH activity on workers and the competence of such services.

Which Type?

Which type of delivery will suit your working? You do not want to duplicate medical checks; neither do you want to break the law by not having the correct processes in place. After all medical services are expensive.

Choosing an OH service

First, be clear about what tasks need addressing, who else will be involved in the work and what you expect the OH service to do.

The task could be about the medical assessment of people starting work or returning to work after illness. Be clear, in what you require, not just the medical assessment but also the legal situation.

What are your other health and safety advisers already contributing? What benefit do you expect from the OH service? The OH service you purchase needs to know about construction generally and what the main health issues are.

Second, having established what contribution you want from the service, choose one to work with you. You can do this by inviting tenders, or by direct recruitment. You may want to take advice from other construction companies. However, you go about it be clear on the specific skills and competencies you want and check they have them.

Contracted OH Services

Contracted OH services have a tenuous position in construction. They too will be "subbies;" for although OH services can offer any health service to construction workers and management – they can only provide what they are asked to provide. They can suggest services and tell the PC what is required, but if they do - risk accusations of "up-selling" or trying to get more money from the contract.

In-House OH Services

In-house OH services provide bespoke services for your workers and are always on hand to assist management with health issues occurring. The downside is the competence and focus of such a service; service level agreements are rarely agreed and in place. Many in-house services do their own thing with little external auditing of performance and compliance.

Where to Find Accredited OH Services

1. The Safe Effective Quality Occupational Health Services (bit.ly/2gB53sJ) or SEQOHS is a government recommended service, which verifies and guarantees OH services and their credentials for providing OH services. The public list is available on the SEQOHS site (bit.ly/2qodI2B).
2. You can also do the same on the Constructing Better Health site (bit.ly/2qnMdWT); here you find construction specific OH services verified b
3. COPHA (bit.ly/2gCsRfF) is a not-for-profit association of OH providers although not specifically for the construction industry

Pick Your Contractor

1. Add your postcode to the search box on one of the above websites to find local and national OH services
2. Pick three services by visiting their websites to see if they provide the types of service you are looking for
3. Set out what you require, such as health surveillance, drug and alcohol testing or cholesterol testing and contact each of the three chosen services via the contact details?
4. Ask for quotes for services

Professional limitations

All medical practitioners must maintain the confidentiality of any medical information they hold, which means that while the occupational physician can advise employers on, for example, an individual's fitness to work or on possible ill-health effects, they are not allowed to provide employers with full medical details on the individual, without the worker's consent.

Some health checks need special qualifications from your OH service, such as:

♦ High-risk health activities such as lead, asbestos, compressed air, ionising radiation
♦ Tests for those working with vibrating tools

Top Tips for Hiring Medical Services

♦ Ask other similar or local organisations who have OH for recommendations of an excellent service or consider sharing services
♦ Ask for references from any potential OH service or individual and ask for website access and leaflets. Look at their marketing literature, which explains what the OH service does--if you understand their messages, the chances are they are mindful of their customers
♦ Set out any special arrangements that are important; for example, if you work shifts, night staff, or home workers; how will they be included

- What happens if the service cancels a clinic on site?
- Do not be afraid to ask for cost reduction strategies such as price matching or reductions for a longer term contract (such as five years instead of three)
- Agree on the logistics of the health clinics as well as the testing and appointment system for your workers (e.g., time, place, disability access if applicable, any special considerations).
- Agree on payment arrangements, contact details, hypothetical situations and expectations
- Set up a service level agreement if possible, setting out all your requirements
- Agree on long-term arrangements and regular meetings/telephone calls to review services
- Review the complaints procedures. Does it have a named contact if things go wrong?
- Have a nominated person who understands the contract, health risk assessment and has some authority in your organisation to run the OH contract going forward. Without this, your OH service and therefore the health of your employees may suffer.

MUST-DO STEPS: Before You Start a Medical Service

- Ask the OH service to provide training programmes for managers--the service cannot and will not be successful without their understanding and cooperation.
- Arrange training for all your supervisory staff and explain how the service will work. Be clear on the types of issues you want OH to deal with.
- Tell employees about the new service and the benefits it will bring; otherwise, they may view an appointment with OH as a disciplinary measure.

Cost of an OH service

Tax Rules

There are definite circumstances when you can get tax relief on expenditure for medical and other services for employees. _The tax rules and the purchase of occupational health support_ (bit.ly/2x5pfJi) are available from the HSE site.

How Much Will OH Work Cost[5]?

The current daily rate for a professional contracted OH worker is approximately:

- ♦ £300 a day for a technician
- ♦ £400 a day for a nurse (without the OH qualification/previous experience)
- ♦ £700 a day for a qualified/experienced OH nurse advisor
- ♦ Up to £3,000 a day for a senior fully qualified OH physician or doctor

A specialist, niche or expert provider could charge more in any sector. Most OH providers have different price ranges depending on where the employee is seen (i.e., on or off-site, in a mobile unit or corporate offices).

Don't forget to consider the following factors as well:

- ♦ Travel time, travel expenses, follow-up procedures, parking, etc., as these can add to the cost of service.
- ♦ For an in-house OH service, salary ranges from £35,000– £40,000 per annum (plus employment costs and ongoing training) depending on location and experience (for a nurse practitioner)
- ♦ OH doctors are usually part-time to reduce costs

---

[5] Estimated in September 2017

Service Level Agreements

Once terms are agreed, the service should be explicitly set out in a service level agreement (SLA) or contract, which also contains agreed-upon targets that your service promises to achieve. For example, it might include, 'I will send a report back to management within five working days after a display screen equipment assessment' or 'HR will be responsible for setting up all appointments'.

Priced by Time or Item

Consider whether to ask for the cost of a health check--for example, an LGV driver medical for £150 (must be signed by a doctor, hence the high charge)--as opposed to a daily rate. Often the daily or half-day price will be more economical.

Retainers

Annual retainers for medical services are an ideal solution if you only need medical advice occasionally or in an emergency. The benefit to you is that you get preferential treatment and an immediate response to any query.

Further Advice and Resources

- Example of a service level agreement (bit.ly/2h05uwS)
- Improving attendance (bit.ly/2x0k51D)
- A Manager's Guide to Occupational Health (bit.ly/2x0reiw) with video
- Read my book The Manager's Ultimate Guide to Health and Wellbeing where I cover many work health issues in greater detail
- What is Occupational Health
- Questions you can ask Occupational Health

30. Health Checks

The three categories of health checks that employers can purchase are set out below in priority order (must, should and could do). If you have a limited budget, focus on health surveillance only, as

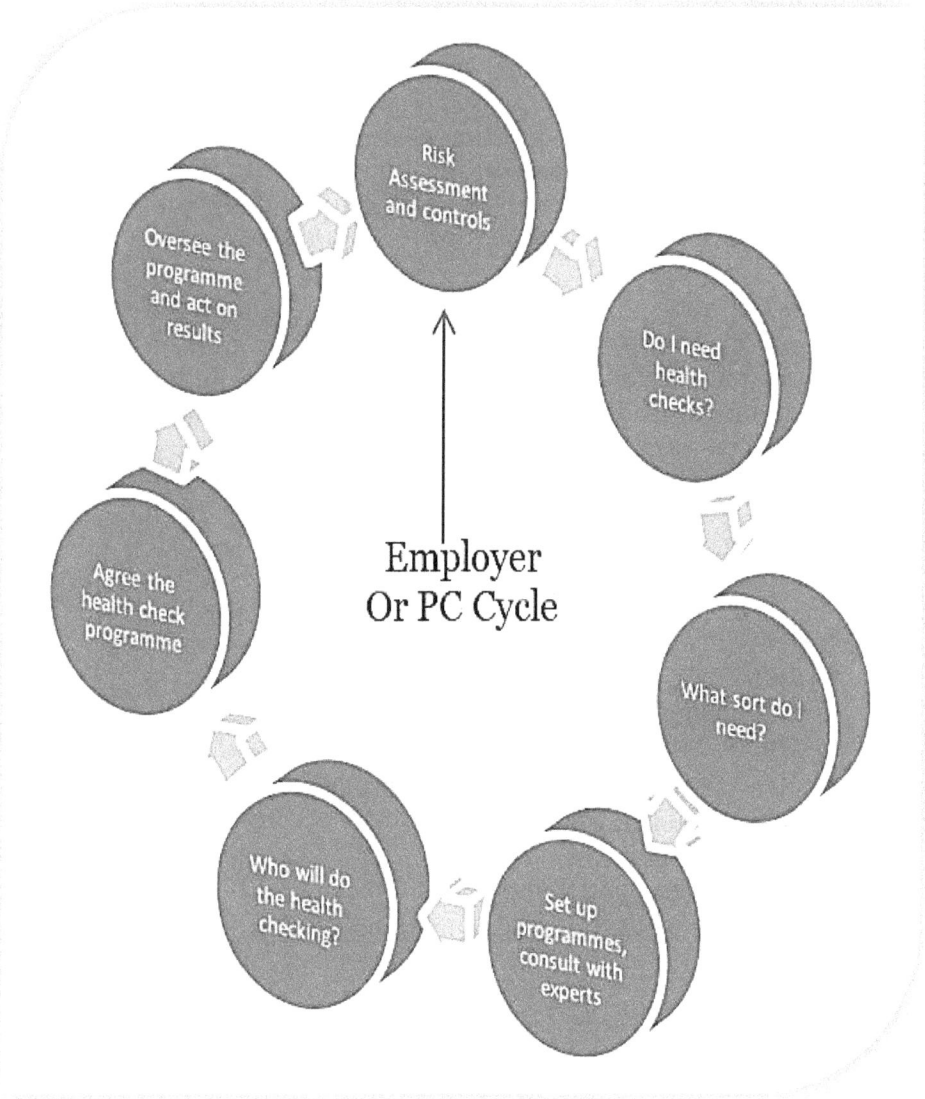

Risk Assessment and controls

Oversee the programme and act on results

Do I need health checks?

Agree the health check programme

Employer Or PC Cycle

What sort do I need?

Who will do the health checking?

Set up programmes, consult with experts

these are the health checks required by law.

30.1 Health Surveillance (Must Do)

Health and safety laws state that workers must have their health monitored if they are at risk of developing a health problem linked to their work (called health surveillance). This identifies any work-related issues, and if the employer/PC acts on tightening up the controls, it will protect all the other workers too.

Start a programme of health checks wherever there are significant health risks to workers, AND there is a relevant health test. I make this point because there isn't always a test available, for example, there is no way to predict if someone will get a bad back or a scientific way of assessing the state of someone's mental health.

Employee's attendance for health surveillance is mandatory where a risk assessment shows it is required.

Health Records

Whenever health surveillance is needed a health record of exposure and results of health checks should be kept by the employer (or PC if they are sponsoring the health checking programme) for each employee. The health record contains basic information for tracking over the years.

As you can see from the example, health records are different from medical records as they do not contain confidential medical information, merely a history of exposures and whether the person is fit to continue working.

In my dealings with all industries but particularly in construction, I have found the health record to be an elusive mystery. Health records were started for statistical purposes so that if a new disease emerged, researchers could look back and track a workers exposure. However, in all my days as an OH professional, I have never had to provide them for either the employer or the visiting HSE inspectors and, in my opinion, need reconsidering.

As the requirement is in regulations such as COSHH, then the employer (not your occupational health provider) must keep health records for each employee for 40 years from the date of last entry. Some regulations - for lead, asbestos, ionising radiation and compressed air - ask for more extended periods (up to 50 years) as ill health effects might not emerge for a significant period after exposure.

W

Health Record

Name		Address	
Nat Ins No		Date of starting employment	
Managers Name		Department	
First			
Second			
Third			
Health Risk Exposures		Dates of Exposures	
Date/Type of Health Surveillance	Outcome	Date Recall Due	Adjustments advised

Further Advice and Resources

♦ Record keeping (bit.ly/2tQvGeY) from the HSE
♦ Control of Substances Hazardous to Health ACOP (bit.ly/2vBR1N9) from the HSE
♦ Managing for Health and Safety (HSG 65) (bit.ly/2Db8C2p) from the HSE

30.2 Fitness for Work (Should Do)

Many of the large construction companies insist that high-risk workers (mostly called safety-critical workers although this term is 'borrowed' from the rail industry) have a full health check to make sure they are not going to harm anyone because of their own poor health (the most common term for this is fitness for work or pre-placement medicals). Yet, these workers may only be on site for a few days – so checking the health of say, a lorry driver who makes a delivery, is going to be costly and time-consuming and will very likely not happen.

Also, different construction companies have different standards of health requirements. An example of this is drug testing: there are many drugs you can test for, the more you choose, the more expensive the screening will be, so you end up having variations from contractor to contractor and from site to site.

Also, consider fitness for work health checks before workers start a new job or after an illness or accident. The purpose is to check that the person is fully fit to work there.

The most commonly applied health standards in construction at the time of writing (July 2017) is the Construction Better Health standards (version 2) which are subject to review and rewrite later in 2017.

30.3 General Health Checks – Health Promotion/Wellbeing (Could do)

Whilst there is no legal requirement for general health checks such as measurements of cholesterol or weight as part of a health promotion or wellbeing campaign, many companies now offer general health checks as well as focussing on work-related health.

Health promotion offers workers the opportunity to say, have their blood pressure checked. Or hear advice on how to stop smoking or lose weight; or, most importantly, if a serious health problem is discovered advised to see their own GP for treatment.

These general health checks are my particular bugbear because employers or PC's opt for this instead of the medicals needed to protect workers health (health surveillance). What you get are terrific general health checks such as blood pressure and cholesterol, which, by the way, freely provided by the NHS, on workers who then work in clouds of dust, high volume noise and hand-held vibratory tools.

Further Advice and Resources

♦ Health surveillance (bit.ly/1ESZ8BM) from the HSE
♦ Is health surveillance required (bit.ly/2s5MuPc) in my workplace? HSE website
♦ Record keeping (bit.ly/2tQvGeY) from the HSE
♦ Constructing Better Health Construction Industry Standards version 2 (bit.ly/2tQv7Sg) for members only

31. Preplacement Health Screening

Employment law in the UK makes it illegal to use medical tests or questions as a means of stopping candidates from getting a job.[6] If you need to make health enquiries, these enquiries must be AFTER an offer of employment.

Many employers are confused about when to ask capability questions because if say, a crane operator can't bear working at heights then the interviewer (and the candidate), need to explore this from a practical point of view. Because of the difficulty, employers have in recruiting and acting fairly in this area, guidance is available from the Gov UK website (bit.ly/2pBBz1n) and sets out exactly what you can and can't discuss in job interviews.

Unfortunately changing the name and the process has not taken away the belief that the OH professionals decide whether people can or can't do a job, that is, applicants are fit or unfit for work. This is not the case, in my career having done hundreds of health checks; I can tell you that only one or two applicants were ever medically unfit for a job. Most applicants are fully fit for the job, and some need minor adjustments, e.g. spectacles or blood pressure medication.

Pre-placement health screening is like a risk assessment on an individual, ensuring the job fits the individual with necessary or reasonable adjustments, rather than the commonly held assumption that it's to exclude workers. Although for high-risk roles there may be issues, where health may compromise safety, and then a balanced view is required and perhaps modified work.

In low-risk work (administration, call centre staff) preplacement screening can be as simple as signing a health declaration which a suitably trained person checks for known health problems or

---

[6] (2010). Equality Act: firms must not ask job applicants about health. Available at bit.ly/2pBWodn

adjustments required. The questions to ask in low-risk occupations are set out in Table 1

Table: Simple Non-Confidential Health Questionnaire

1	Do you need any special adaptations or aids to assist you at work whether or not you have a disability?	Yes	No
2	Are you having or waiting for treatment or investigations of any kind at present?	Yes	No
3	Do you or have you ever had any health problems, which have been caused or made worse by your work?	Yes	No
If applicant answers 'yes' to any of the above, do not inquire into the reasons but make an appointment for them to see the Occupational Health Doctor or Nurse to have a full discussion			
Signed:	Dated:		

Pre-placement health screening is for:

+ Establishing baseline health records (useful for measuring health when starting a new job and before exposure to health risks)
+ Identifying reasonable adjustments to the work or the working environment
+ Explaining specific health risks and requirements for each job
+ Complying with health and safety procedures, e.g., demonstrating how to insert earplugs, advice on hazards such as asbestos and construction dust
+ Changing of work role, e.g., from low-risk work to a safety critical role

- Introducing new workers to the health and safety culture of your business
- Assessing specific groups of workers, e.g., pregnant, young workers, asthmatics
- For some jobs, there are legal duties to do health checks, e.g., those working with lead or compressed air.
- Most construction employers carry out pre-placement screening on high-risk jobs (also called safety critical)

Meaningful pre-placement health screening depends on the initial health and safety risk assessment setting out the requirements of the job, mitigation of health risks where possible and identifying areas of high risk. With this information, pre-placement health screening can begin.

The Equality Act makes it clear that employers have to be careful about asking health-related questions either prior to or in an interview; as there is still prejudice and ignorance about health conditions and the effect on work, especially in relation to mental health. Make sure you only ask about specific health AFTER a job offer, or you could face charges of discrimination.

The process of pre-placement health screening is set out in Flow Chart2.

Further Advice and Resources

- The Good Practice Guide on Medical Fitness for Plant Operators (bit.ly/2pBU1Hg)
- See Chapter 36 on Equality and Disability
- See flow chart (next page) for information

Preplacement Health Screening

Health and safety risk assessment of proposed job/post.
Categorise as:
1. Low, medium, high risk role
2. Safety critical or fitness for task required
3. Health surveillance/regular health checks required

Job offer made to applicant with duties explained.

| Low Risk (E.g. Administration, call centres) | Med/High Risk Health and medical surveillance required | Job Specific Fitness checks required e.g. safety critical, drivers, night workers |

Signed health declaration returned to employer

Confidential health questionnaire completed for occupational health services to assess

All OK

Health issues declared

Assessed by occupational health

Fit for work with no adjustments required

Fit for work with regular health reviews/health surveillance

Specified adjustments required to the workplace/work or an operational assessment*

The employer must make the final decision of whether to employ or not, based on health assessment, recommendations and the operational assessment outcomes

*Operational Assessment
This type of 'on the job' assessment is needed if there is doubt about a workers capability to work safely. It takes place in controlled or test conditions by an assessor who has knowledge of job to be done and understand health and safety implications. It ensures workers can demonstrate reliable and safe working.
The assessor records an outcome of (1) satisfactory, (2) unsatisfactory or (3) satisfactory with restrictions.

32. Attendance Management

Why do some people want to come back to work the next day after a heart attack and others take a week off with a cold? How people feel and believe about their health can affect their behaviour and recovery from health problems such as a back injury or resuming movement after an operation.

Other issues which affect health and recovery, are the personal health factors such as an underlying health issue which could affect healing (immune diseases or long-term chest conditions) or complications after surgery such as a wound infection. The manager may not be aware of these issues and wonder about the employee's motivation to return to work.

Logic too is obscured when an organisations' culture comes into play; none more so than from the macho culture observed in many construction companies where the emergence of mental health issues has taken many of us by surprise.

People react differently to different health events and managers struggle with the right strategy especially with the introduction of the fit note, replacing the sick note back in 2010.

The main difference between the two is that Doctors formerly only had two options - workers were either fit or not fit for work. The problem with this approach is that many businesses can offer modified duties; it's just that no one ever officially asked. With the new process, workers can stay at work, meaning they are productive and the business is not losing one of their workers but, as we shall see, whether or not you offer modified work etc., really depends on the job and the health condition.

All about Fit Notes

The 'fit note' is the informal name for the 'Statement of Fitness for Work' that replaced the 'sick note' in April 2010.

The fit note now has many more options for the GP to tick:

1. Not fit for work is still one option; however,
2. Offers 'may be fit for work' takes into account the following:
   I. Phased return
   II. Altered hours
   III. Amended duties
   IV. Workplace adaptations

Within each of the 'Maybe Fit For Work' sections the GP can make suggestions on what work would be suitable, thus keeping the worker at work, or help the worker return to work sooner.

The assessment of whether your employee is or isn't fit for work or may be fit for work (and any written instruction on the fit note), is advice, and you as the manager have the right to accept or deny the recommendations from the GP.

Many workers do not understand this point of view, believing that a GP has the statutory right to tell a workplace what to do. You, as a manager, have the power to override what the GP or specialist suggests, taking into account the needs of your business.

This needs carefully explaining to the misguided worker and is useful information to share with workers prior to seeing their GP.

In my experience, if an employee is going to see their GP to talk about their health and fitness with a view to going off sick or after illness, serious accident or long-term absence; the best results come from talking to the worker to discuss the work options available before they see their GP.

If you have a worker information portal such as a website, why not put the information there.

GP's too, generally appreciate any help from the workplace on what options are available.

Overruling A GP or Fit Note

Joe comes into work brandishing a fit note stating that he can only do office work and his regular job is as a scaffolder. What do you do?

Government Advice is clear:

'The assessment about whether your employee is not fit for work or may be fit for work (and any other advice in the fit note) is classed as advice, and it is for employers to determine whether or not to accept it. Occasionally, you may believe that your employee is not fit for work when they have been assessed as fit for work by their doctor, or you may think that your employee could do some work when they have been assessed as 'not fit for work' by their doctor..... In situations like this, you as the employer are within your rights to gather other evidence about your employee's fitness for work from other doctors or healthcare professionals. You can choose to give this other evidence precedence over the advice in the fit note.[7]*'*

If you decide to overrule or ignore the advice though, be sure you have business reasons why you can't accommodate the recommendations. And, if you have access to medical professionals, always ask their advice and ALWAYS consider whether the worker is disabled; meaning you will need to consider how you can adapt the workplace to suit, as set out in the Equality Act.

Sickness

All of us at some stage in our lives will experience ill-health. How a manager deals with vulnerable workers can have a long-standing effect on the subsequent relationship with an employer.

Managers and employers need people to do their job, keep the wheels turning and keep a business going. Employees are paid to work, and when they are off sick, for whatever reason, they are not

---

[7] Fit for Work: *Guidance for Employers, free download* (bit.ly/2pCHR13)

fulfilling their contract of employment, whether they receive company sick pay or not.

Also, contractors need their subcontractors to turn up on time. Without the correct type and number of workers, business or projects could fail. So for employers and clients, it is imperative that workers come to work, bearing in mind the penalties for being late with delivery of a project and non-attendance of critical workers.

Statistics about Absence from Work

- ◆ Studies show that the longer people are off work due to sickness, the more likely it is that they will never return to work
- ◆ Other illnesses occur whilst people are away long term, due to isolation and lack of social interaction (e.g., depression and anxiety)
- ◆ After only six weeks' sickness absence, a person's ability to return to work falls away, and 1 in 5 will never return to their original job.

Most people who permanently leave work are suffering from mild to moderate mental health issues or muscle, joint or back pain - not severe and incurable health conditions.

There is another side to this argument; research shows that work is essential for good health and wellbeing for individual workers too.

Managing Absence in Construction

Sickness absence on construction sites is complex. Many of the larger employers have very few employed or 'white collar' workers where there are few issues with absence. However, on-site supervisors have to deal with the fallout from the absence of their contractors, which means the on-site manager may have to step in to:

- ♦ Manage the worker's absence
- ♦ Undertake the return to work interview
- ♦ Deal with fit notes
- ♦ Set up rehabilitation programmes
- ♦ Monitor performance of sick or potentially sick workers
- ♦ Encourage attendance

The involvement of the on-site supervision will largely depend on the relationship the subcontractor has with the contractor.

Contact when Sick

For employers, keeping in contact is a crucial factor in all of the above points; without contact, you will not be able to deal with the return to work and fulfil your legal obligations under health and safety legislation.

Listed below are some dos and don'ts to help you deal with those off sick:

Do:

- ♦ Create a climate of trust by agreeing methods, frequency and reasons for keeping in contact
- ♦ Consider the timing and form of communications and who should make them
- ♦ Be flexible, treat each case individually but on a fair and consistent basis
- ♦ Keep a note of contacts made
- ♦ Welcome workers back to work after absence
- ♦ Carry out return to work interviews (see below for more details)
- ♦ Give workers an opportunity to discuss their health or other concerns that affect their performance or attendance in private
- ♦ Remember, some tablets and treatments affect performance, such as physical stamina, mood, driving, machinery operation and safety-critical tasks

- Encourage absent employees to talk to their own GP or the occupational health service, about what they may be able to do as they make progress or adjust to their condition.

Don't:

- Wait until someone has been off for weeks before making contact
- Delay making contact or pass responsibility to someone else, unless unavoidable
- Make assumptions or listen to gossip about a worker's situation or their medical circumstances. Do find out directly from the worker
- Talk to other people about a worker's details without their knowledge and consent
- Forget that recovery times vary from person to person

Return to Work After Sickness

'Return to work' interviews are an essential tool for managing absence. It might be an informal chat to welcome an employee back to work, and confirm their record of absence is correct. Or it could be a discussion of remaining health issues with the potential to affect employment and any adjustments needed, which is essential if the worker has a high-risk job.

Traditionally managers feel uncomfortable discussing health issues in detail especially with members of the opposite sex or if the perceived health issue is embarrassing or likely to cause distress.

A good way of dealing with people in return to work interview scenarios is to use the WARM approach.

WARM Return to Work

'WARM' is an easy way to remember the steps of the return to a work meeting, between you and the person coming back to work. Here are the four stages to cover:

W	Welcome back, be friendly and open, not hostile. Focus on the individual and their wellbeing
A	Absence discussion - look at their annual attendance records, count up days lost, are there patterns such as after a weekend or holiday?
R	Responsibility to attend work - the most often overlooked part. Remind the worker how important they are both in attendance and what their absence means.
M	Move on - update the worker on what has happened in their absence, how this will affect them. Any changes. Discuss a rehabilitation programme if required and suggest ways of helping them return to work in the face of lingering health issues. Also consider a risk assessment if the worker has difficulties e.g., can they evacuate if there is a fire?

Note that tragic circumstances at work, such as an accident or loss of life at work will probably require specialised counselling services.

Gradual or Supervised Return to Work

GP's, the fit for work service or an OH service can recommend a programme of integration back to work, especially after a serious illness or injury.

This will:

- Recommend what the worker can do in the short term
- Speed up recovery
- Retain the worker's input and skills, especially for key roles such as supervisors and engineers
- Remove barriers to return to work.

Keeping in contact with your absent employee will help you to plan any adjustments to their work needed for their return. Some modifications may also be necessary to enable employees with a health condition that could worsen over time, to stay in post.

Further Advice and Resources

- Return to Work Interview (bit.ly/2uNeDhh)
- See also Chapter 33 for advice on counselling and EAP's
- See Chapter 36 on Equality and Disability

33. Referring Workers to a Medical Service

If managers have concerns about the health of a worker, especially if it affects their performance or safety; a specialist health adviser can help by talking to the worker, assessing the impact of their health on work and giving the business expert advice and guidance; the process is called a management referral.

The individuals' GP, while understanding the health issues and their patient, may not understand the work processes or the hazards present in the workplace. More importantly though is the patient/Doctor relationship which is based on the GP being supportive of their patient, making decisions about employment is challanging here, due to conflicting interests between the work and health.

An independent medical assessment from an occupational health (OH) service is a way of obtaining a work-focused, objective and medically competent opinion, which is crucial when work is high risk, where long-term capability is in question or the situation overlaid with domestic issues and conflicts with management.

How Referrals Help

OH services usually deal with questions such as:

- ♦ Is he/she fit to undertake/return to their job?
- ♦ Is there an underlying medical condition to account for this high level of sickness absence?
- ♦ Is it likely that the Equality Act 2010 will apply?
- ♦ When will he/she be fit to undertake full duties?
- ♦ What sort of work adjustments are necessary to help this person stay at work?
- ♦ Is this level of absence likely to continue?
- ♦ Is there more help or support we can offer?

Managers/employers start by discussing the problem health issue with their employee and how a referral to OH will help manage their situation. Following discussions, the referral papers are sent to the OH service who will set up an appointment with the worker.

If employees refuse to cooperate with the referral process, and they are within their rights to do so, you need to explain to the worker, that decisions have to be made without the benefit of professional objective health advice.

The Appointment

Depending on how the contract is set up with OH, the appointment can be either face to face or over the phone. Telephone or video calling has become increasingly popular; it cuts down on travel time and is usually more convenient. However, some health conditions are best dealt with face to face and may not be amenable to telephone discussions, e.g. work-related stress or impairment where a physical examination is required.

During the OH appointment/discussion, the worker and OH discuss:

- The role of both and responsibilities of OH and the manager
- Health issues relevant to work
- Difficulties with work due to the health issue
- The course of the illness and prognosis, medication
- How much information the OH service can share with the manager
- Possible solutions for the health issue, e.g., return to work plans
- The response to the questions posed by the worker's manager on the referral papers
- Any follow up or review
- Whether to write to their GP/Specialist
- Implications of any recommendations
- Possible outcomes from the recommendations

Benefits of Management Referrals

♦ All discussions are medical 'in confidence' unless the worker gives their consent for the medical information to be released. The final report and recommendations will be discussed with the worker and usually consent obtained to release the report to management.

♦ Personal health issues under the Data Protection Act are classed as 'sensitive' in nature, so confidentiality in the workplace is important to keep within the law and to keep your employee's trust.

♦ Many workers find the consultation of great benefit, not only to talk to another health professional but advice usually covers alternative methods of treatments and reassurance.

♦ The recommendations after the assessment aim to help both the employer and worker to negotiate a way through the situation without causing too much disruption or further injury to the worker.

♦ Under the Health and Safety at Work etc. Act 1974 (bit.ly/2pBpLMA), all businesses should ensure the general health and safety of their staff and those affected by their work: companies that hire medical experts, show they take this duty seriously.

The report from occupational health will answer the questions asked and contain recommendations for the employer to consider, such as a phased return to work after an absence and/or work adjustments. It is the employer's decision of whether to accept the independent medical recommendations - although if the worker is disabled the employer would be expected to make reasonable adjustments to comply with the Equality Act.

Steps of the Management Referral Process

If you've invested in medical support for your construction company, you need to use it correctly, or you could be adding to your problems rather than solving them, especially when using a management referral service.

This section sets out five critical steps that will super-charge your manager referral process, and why they are vital for bypassing mistakes. It also shows you how to avoid getting an unworkable recommendation back from occupational health (OH); or if you do get one, show you how to rescue the situation.

I Need to Make a Management Referral

You've identified an employee with a health problem, such as:

1. Three health-related absences in any six month period
2. Emerging patterns of absence, e.g. Mondays and Fridays
3. Any stress, anxiety or depression related absence
4. Any musculo-skeletal related absence
5. Any absence exceeding five days with no return to work date identified
6. A health issue affecting performance, or there has been a workplace accident thought due to poor health

You need to figure out what advice you need and why - as well as discussing the situation with your worker.

Discussion with Worker

To get the best results from the management referral process, follow these steps carefully:

1. Explain precisely the reason for referral and ask employee to sign the referral form to show that they understand why they need to attend OH
2. Let workers know what questions you need answering and why it's important
3. Tell the worker about the system of referral and how it works for both your and their benefit
4. Give the worker an information sheet or website address where they can read about how the company OH works and contact details, so they can call if they have a query before the appointment. Stress the confidentiality of the OH process
5. If the employee agrees, send the referral form to OH. Remember workers can refuse to attend

How Did the Report Come About?

OH writes a report after reading your referral form, examining and speaking with the worker, looked at the job description and occasionally getting a report from the GP or specialist. They then make recommendations based on their experience and training, helping you manage the worker and the health issue.

Let's go back and look at how you can prevent poor outcomes.

Step 1: The OH Contract

All services should be set up with a service level agreement (SLA) specifying how the OH service will work. The SLA will also cover the process for reporting to you. Many OH services have options for discussing a situation with the line manager before writing the report, which is good practice, especially with complex cases.

Make it clear to your worker, from the start, that it is the manager's responsibility to make any decisions on the recommendations from OH. OH has no authority to make employment decisions.

One example of how this is applied is in cases of disability (under the Equality Act). Although the OH doctor or nurse can give an opinion on whether the person is disabled, the final decision will always be the employer's [8]

Step 2: Discussion with the Employee/Worker

In most cases, you want to find if a worker can't or won't do the job, which is why you use the management referral service; you need an expert, independent, medical opinion.

What you don't want to do is to view the process as a tick box exercise before dismissal or the disciplinary process; everyone sees your motives there. No matter what the recommendations are

---

[8] See *Gallop v Newport City Council* (bit.ly/2eQYYVh)

from OH, some managers ignore them entirely and go straight to the dismissal. The management referral to OH is merely a step along the way, making the referral process of doubtful value to your workers.

The most significant issue, though, is when the employee and the manager have different versions of the truth, which is difficult in cases of bullying, harassment and stress at work.

Although the worker has the opportunity to talk to the OH doctor or nurse, the only information OH has from you, the manager is on the written referral form. In my experience, managers write down the minimal on the referral form and tend to leave out relevant facts. I'm not sure if it's due to time pressures or not knowing what is needed for the management referral. In some cases, it is because the manager does not want to put the full story. Whatever the reason, it means that the discussions with the worker at OH are different to what is on the referral form, resulting in the employees explaining the situation from their perspective and overriding the manager's concerns.

Managers, if you want a meaningful report back from OH, always write down the relevant facts of the case or be open with the employee about the reasons for referral and questions you want to be answered.

If you think the case is complicated, or hijacked by the employee:

- ♦ Talk to OH before the appointment to clarify any problematic issues that are likely to come up.
- ♦ Add your contact details to the referral so OH can call you to clarify points before they write their report. Any written statement becomes discoverable in law, so it's important to clarify any disputed facts before writing.

Step 3: Receiving the Report

OH discusses and agrees on the final report with the employee during the consultation. An excellent report will summarise the health issues and give you clear recommendations of how to deal with the situation. If you get a report that is unclear, contains errors or doesn't ask the questions you have asked; contact the author of the report immediately and discuss (rationally) how and where the report fails.

Satisfactory Report Received

From the recommendations, you will see the best way to deal with your employee's health issues. If it's rehabilitation or a phased return to work programme, you will have an outline of progress and checkpoints you need to make.

Unsatisfactory Report Received

The report from OH does not deal with the situation and/or the recommendations are unworkable. You may be angry and disappointed, but aside from that, you have to deal with the situation. Take my advice on this: it is not OH's intention to cause problems for you or the worker.

Do not discuss the report with the worker at this stage! That will confuse him or her and undermine any good that the management referral might do.

If you disagree with the recommendations, think about why. Is it that:

- ♦ The recommendations are nothing like you expected--they go too far or not far enough?
- ♦ You are reacting to somebody else trying to control your team?
- ♦ You believe the worker is trying to get one over on you?
- ♦ The OH person is incapable of making a business decision and is too soft and fluffy?
- ♦ The report is confusing, and you are not sure what to do next?

Step 4: Feedback and Negotiations

If the report has factual errors or is unhelpful, make an appointment to talk or see the author of the report and ask for a correction. It may be obvious to you, but explain why the recommendations are unworkable and suggest alternatives built on what's in the report already. Or maybe you have another solution?

You and the OH professional must try to reach an agreement. If you agree, ask that they change their recommendation to show your discussion in the report.

It may be that there are no other options possible, so this needs acknowledging too.

Note: Although health professionals are unable to disclose the nature of illness, it is still possible to discuss capabilities without going into detail of the health issue.

Informing the Employee about Changes

Because the OH practitioner has spoken to the employee about the original report and recommendations, he or she will need telling of any changes made after the discussion. Often managers get upset at this point, believing I am asking the employee if it's OK to change things. But it is not about getting the employee's agreement; it's about explaining what happened and the suggested solutions. OH professionals would quickly lose credibility in your organisation if word spread that I said one thing to the worker and another to a manager.

Step 5: Case Conference

If a case has gone pear-shaped or you think it has the potential to do so, consider arranging a case conference--after the OH sees the employee.

Case conference usually involves the OH practitioner, an HR representative and the manager to discuss the way forward together. It is also an excellent practice to invite an individual's trade union or worker representative. Open meetings prevent misunderstandings and delays; decisions are immediate and recorded for planning purposes.

In my experience, case conferences are rare, but when they happen, successful.

Managing Repeated Short-Term Sickness

Managers agree, dealing with workers who have excessive occasional sick days off is more difficult than controlling long-term absence. Random days absences here and there are unpredictable and happen at short notice. The remaining workers pick up the duties of those off sick, which results in work overload for them, as well as missed deadlines for the business.

Medical Assessment

For those who have poor sickness record, it is legitimate to ask occupational health (OH) to assess the worker's overall health for guidance on how to help with improving attendance (see Management Referral above). It may be that there is an undiscovered or incorrectly treated health problem and the worker should be advised to seek further treatment.

In construction, many workers will not have registered with a GP, so this type of advice is useful for those working away from home or have not registered with a Doctor.

Conclusion

Managers need a good system of referral, with clear arrangements. They also need to be transparent and willing to accommodate workers as well as capable of deciding when to draw the line.

Use these five steps, and you'll be amazed how much more useful and efficient the management referral process will be for you and your workers. Plus you will be getting the best from your medical support service.

Further Advice and Resources

- Guidance on the Equality Act (bit.ly/2pBAQxd)
- See Chapter 36 on Equality and Disability
- Example of service level agreement with key performance indicators (bit.ly/2gCj1dU) to adapt
- How to Refer to OH (video) (youtu.be/On6Ao2A7t70)
- General advice on the management referral process (bit.ly/2gAu9Ik)
- Referral forms, consent and templates (bit.ly/2xybx23) available on Working Well Solutions but you will need to register

34. Other Professional Health Services

34.1 Physiotherapy

Musculo-skeletal injuries are top of the list for work-related absence and any service that helps workers to return or stay at work after an injury, can pay for themselves many times over. Physiotherapy assesses an injury, reassures the injured person (this addresses the individual's underlying anxiety), and assists with rehabilitation.

Physiotherapy helps to restore movement and function after injury, illness or disability; plus reduces the risk of injury or illness in the future; used for:

◆ Bones, joints and soft tissue – such as back pain (bit.ly/2qYZaXk), neck pain (bit.ly/2qYWusG), shoulder pain (bit.ly/2qZa8fu) and sports injuries (bit.ly/2skQBu6)
◆ Brain or nervous system – such as movement problems resulting from a stroke (bit.ly/2r6qL98o)
◆ Heart and circulation – such as rehabilitation after a heart attack (bit.ly/2r6slb5)
◆ Lungs and breathing – such as chronic obstructive pulmonary disease (COPD) (bit.ly/2r6m3bo)

Physiotherapy improves physical activity while helping prevent further injuries.

What physiotherapists do

Some of the main approaches used by physiotherapists include:

◆ Education and advice – general information about proper posture and correct lifting or carrying techniques
◆ Exercises to improve general health and mobility, and to strengthen specific body parts or muscle groups

- Using their hands to help relieve pain and stiffness, and to encourage better movement of the body

Hiring a Physiotherapist

Physiotherapy is available through the NHS or privately. Many companies employ sessional physiotherapists as the waiting lists for NHS treatment are long.

Read more about accessing physiotherapy through the NHS (bit.ly/2slleQ8) and other means.

Physiotherapy services can be contracted on a daily, weekly, monthly or 'as required' basis and many will hold clinics on site to allow workers easier access. Providers of services vary in size from large multi-nationals to independent consultants running their own businesses. Other widely used treatments of musculo-skeletal problems include chiropractors and osteopaths.

Further Advice and Resources

- The Chartered Society of Physiotherapists (bit.ly/2r6O4ji) offers free exercise leaflets on back pain, tennis elbow, etc.
- British Chiropractic Association (bit.ly/2slcYiQ)
- General Osteopathic Council (bit.ly/2slqKSy)

34.2 Counselling/EAP

EAP

An employee assistance programme (EAP) is a work programme designed to assist productivity and attendance issues at work by supporting workers who have personal problems that affect job performance, such as relationships, finance, alcohol, drug and legal matters.

What to look for in an EAP

The essential function of a successful EAP is the ability to provide confidential support services, on demand when they are needed and free of charge for employees.

EAPs usually have access to a wide range of services and support functions where workers can be signposted or referred directly.

All users of the EAP service do so voluntarily, although many accept referrals from line managers or HR, which helps for those who are nervous about contacting an external service.

Discuss how you want an EAP to operate with your company when you set up the contract; taking into account your policies, measures to accommodate data protection, and employee confidentiality.

What does the EAP Offer?

Service usually consists of a blend of the following:

- Money advice and debt management
- Child and elder care information services
- Legal information and guidance
- Information on emotional, work-life and workplace issues
- Assessment, support, short-term counselling and referral for employee issues
- Management referrals and support
- Usage reports (anonymous)
- Management information on employee and organisational interventions
- A website with interactive content and information.
- Consultation and training for managers and supervisors within your organisation

How an EAP Works

The key elements of a full EAP service are:

- ♦ 24-hour telephone support, assessment and counselling services
- ♦ Assessment of needs
- ♦ Short-term (ranges from five to 10 sessions) psychological interventions delivered face to face and/or by telephone
- ♦ Case management and management information
- ♦ Management consultation
- ♦ Website information and services to support the EAP with interactive content, fact sheets and online services

Pricing

There are three main ways to price an EAP

1. Charges are on a 'per capita' basis, calculated on the expected (not actual) use of services
2. An 'as used' pricing method and includes core services, such as telephone counselling, work-life services and web-based services included as a fixed fee. All face-to-face counselling is an additional sum, based on the volume used.
3. Pricing EAPs 'per call' with a set-up fee, and additional costs for marketing and account management. On top of this, the purchaser would pay for any calls to the EAP at a set rate.

Other components available:

- ♦ Marketing literature (annually)
- ♦ Mental health awareness training for managers/groups
- ♦ Management information (e.g., usage, types of issues)
- ♦ Account management meetings
- ♦ Web portal
- ♦ Wellbeing portal[9]

------

[9] Adapted from *UK Buyers Guide of EAP* (bit.ly/2xyO2WL)

Counselling

Counselling services can be part of an EAP or the only support offered by a business to workers. The British Association of Counselling and Psychotherapy (BACP) define counselling as:

'Counselling is a range of talking therapies delivered by trained practitioners over a short or long term, to help them bring about effective change or enhance wellbeing. Counselling is not about giving advice or telling a client to take a particular action. Further, attendance should not adversely affect career progression or status at work and counsellors do not judge or exploit their clients in any way.'

How Does Counselling Work?

Workplace counsellors usually work within a short-term or time-limited framework, often between five and ten sessions - if more sessions are needed the employer has the option to pay for more sessions.

The counsellors have an understanding of organisational cultures and workplace factors that impact on the psychological health of people at work. Service providers can supervise stress audits to help organisations meet their 'duty of care' obligations.

Many businesses offer counselling after a critical incident or trauma for those workers affected by a tragic or disturbing work event.

Models of Counselling Service

1. Internal

Counsellors are employed directly by the organisation and understand the culture of the host organisation. The potential disadvantage is that some clients may prefer a completely separate service, outside their organisation due to concerns about confidentiality.

2. External

An external counselling service provides the service. The advantage is that the service is usually available 24/7. The potential disadvantage is its remoteness from the employer leading to misunderstanding about the policy and culture of their workplace.

3. Hybrid

A hybrid uses a mix of internal and external services. Here, an external provider carries out telephone support but refers to internal counsellors to provide face to face counselling. The advantage is that a combined service builds a better understanding of the organisational culture, whilst bringing flexibility and familiarity. The disadvantage is that the two sides need to cooperate to ensure complete integration.

4. When Needed

If you don't believe workers need a counselling service, can't afford the outlay or want to test the water; engage a suitably qualified freelance or self-employed workplace counsellor on an 'ad hoc' basis. This provides a resource for smaller organisations or where there is limited numbers of referrals.[10]

Cognitive Behaviour Therapy (CBT)

CBT is one of many therapy's available and recommended by NICE[11] as being the most effective, with the rider, 'it is not effective for everyone'.

CBT works on the basis that thoughts, feelings, physical sensations and actions are all interconnected, and negative thoughts and feelings trap you in a vicious cycle. The therapy teaches you to

---

10 Adapted from British Association for Counselling and Psychotherapy Counselling in the Workplace (bit.ly/2pKNfiD)

11 Nice.org.uk. (2009). Depression in adults: recognition and management NICE.

change negative patterns and, in learning to do so, improves the way you feel.

Unlike some other talking treatments, CBT deals with your current problems, rather than focusing on issues from your past. It looks to improve your state of mind on a daily basis.

You can do CBT individually, with groups, or even self-help with a book or computer programme. Sessions are usually once a week or once every two weeks, and lasts between five and 20 sessions, with each session lasting 30-60 minutes.

Further Advice and Resources

- Leaflet on <u>CBT from the Royal College of Psychiatrists</u> (bit.ly/2pKQab3)

34.3 Occupational Hygienist

Occupational hygienists use science and engineering to control risks to health, by designing out hazards and applying engineering controls to reduce exposures to a minimum.

This approach protects workers from serious, and even fatal, illnesses caused by work-related activities.

Examples of typical projects for an occupational hygienist include:

- Conducting a noise survey in a factory to determine noise levels
- Measuring and sampling levels of dust in an aggregates plant or quarry, using specialist equipment to evaluate worker exposure
- Effectively managing the handling of chemical products to prevent ill health conditions such as musculo-skeletal disorders, asthma and dermatitis

Further Advice and Resources

- For more information about hygienists and their work, <u>watch a YouTube video here</u>: (bit.ly/2qIsiCi)
- Find an <u>occupational hygienist</u> (bit.ly/2vC96HU)

34.4 Private Health Care Membership Schemes

The NHS serves the needs of the UK population. However, there is pressure on services meaning the waiting time can be extended in some areas and for some common health problems. This is not a good option when workers are off sick or are struggling to cope with an aspect of their work.

The benefits of private health insurance offers:

- Speedy access to diagnosis and treatment
- Fast track appointments
- Telephone health advice services
- Often other benefits such as gym memberships

The drawbacks of private health insurance:

- The same service is available on the NHS without the wait if it is a severe illness
- It's expensive, and the cost tends to rise over the years
- Chronic illnesses are not usually covered by the basic plan
- The treatment required may not be available in the local area
- Workers can opt out of the service as it is taxable benefit or on ethical grounds
- Benefits are limited to the package the employer buys

Further Advice and Resources

- <u>Private Medical Insurance</u> (bit.ly/2gRLPj1) from the Money Advice Service

35. Review of an OH Service

Perhaps you already have an occupational health (OH) service, and wonder if it is fit for purpose? Are you finding your different sites have different practices? Or are you taking on a contract and wondering if your current service delivers the right sort of health checks for the new health risks involved? You may have misgivings about whether your OH service is doing what it should be, using evidence-based strategies or at least best practice? Is the current service providing value for money, could it do more or less? Or maybe, you don't have any occupational health service at all, and you think perhaps you should?

If these questions are troubling you, you should consider a review of your medical service provision and this section takes you through the steps of analysis.

The type of review you choose for your OH services depends on:

♦ The size of your organisation
♦ The geographical spread of the company and the contracts you work on
♦ How much control you have over contracts
♦ The health risks in the business or contracts
♦ Which laws apply

Who Should do the Review?

It's difficult for an OH service to review their own service for you and few people outside of the profession understand it fully. It is a somewhat closed shop. Your best bet is to opt for an auditor with a neutral perspective and no expectations or personal interest in the review outcome.

Just to make sure we all understand this, occupational health's primary work is **preventing work-related ill health**.

For more information on this go to the HSE website on health surveillance (bit.ly/I9Eggf)

159

This says:

"Health surveillance allows for early identification of ill health and helps identify any corrective action needed. Health surveillance may be required by law if your employees are exposed to noise or vibration, solvents, fumes, dusts, biological agents and other substances hazardous to health, or work in compressed air."

One way of testing understanding of OH matters, within your own organisation, prior to a full OH review, is to survey your managers that use the service, and gauge their responses and expectations.

Use SurveyMonkey (bit.ly/2h6Phm3) and ask your own questions, such as:

◆ Is the current OH service meeting expectations?
◆ Is the service adding value to your work?
◆ Could managers have managed as well by using the individual's GP?
◆ Did you understand the report that OH sent you?
◆ Was the response timely?
◆ Satisfaction scores
◆ How were problems resolved?
◆ What more do you expect of OH?

Limitations of the review

Competent reviewers should do the formal investigation, especially if the current service OH has been in place for years. Even if the general opinion of your medical support is favourable, it may not be doing what it should be.

The higher the health risks in your business, the more critical choosing the right service and review becomes.

Conclusion

From the final review of occupational health services, with recommendations and options, you will be able to decide if your current occupational health service fits your needs or whether you need to reconsider, revamp and reorganise.

And, most importantly, from the workshops, interviews and the process itself, you will have increased awareness and understanding of occupational health issues in your company.

Further Advice and Resources

- Auditing your OH Service (bit.ly/2gT2Idi)
- Guidance on Choosing an OH Provider for Your Organisation (bit.ly/2gT2Idi) by COHPA

36. The Equality Act

The Equality Act (bit.ly/2vqZ9MU) defines disability as:

> *'Having a physical or mental impairment that has a 'substantial' and 'long-term' negative effect on a person's ability to do normal daily activities.'*

For more information on the definition and application to workers, go to the Government website (bit.ly/2rd212t)

If an employee becomes or is disabled, you are legally required under the Equality Act to make reasonable adjustments that will enable people to work with their disability if possible.

What is reasonable depends on:

♦ The financial and other impacts of adjustments on your budget and activities
♦ How effective modifications are likely to be
♦ The particular needs of your individual employee, not the nature of their disability alone
♦ The availability of financial or other help to you

Get into the habit of considering reasonable adjustments to help an employee return to work whether or not they are disabled in the legal sense.

What Are Reasonable Adjustments?

Adjustments need not be huge. It could be something as simple as changing a start time to avoid busy traffic or allocating a small part of a job to someone else. Solutions are often found by working with your employee, or an occupational health service.

The critical steps in planning adjustments are:

♦ Consider what workers can do rather than what they can't

- Assess the possible barriers to the worker's return
- Consider how you adjust the work to overcome these obstacles
- Review health and safety risk assessments in the light of the proposed adjustments
- Review how well the changes work
- Seek professional advice, where necessary, to help you and your employee make informed decisions

Examples of Adjustments to Working Arrangements

- Allow a phased return to contracted working hours or workloads to build up strength and confidence
- Change your employee's working hours to allow more comfortable travel to work, or flexible working to ease work/life balance
- Provide help with transport to and from work
- Arrange home working.
- Allow workers to attend rehabilitation or treatment appointments in work time

Examples of Adjustments to Premises

- Move tasks to more accessible areas and closer to washing and toilet facilities
- Make alterations to premises, e.g., providing a ramp for people who find steps difficult

Examples of Adjustments to a Job

- Provide new or modify existing equipment and tools
- Modify workstations, furniture, and movement patterns
- Provide more training
- Modify instructions, method statements or reference manuals
- Modify work patterns or management systems to cut pressures and give worker more control
- Arrange telephone conferences to reduce travel

- ◆ Modify testing or assessment procedures
- ◆ Provide a buddy or mentor while the worker regains their confidence
- ◆ Reallocate work to others temporarily
- ◆ Provide alternative employment

Risk Assessment

Under health and safety law, you have to undertake a risk assessment of your activities to prevent harm. If there has been a significant change in an employee's capability due to illness, injury or disability making them more vulnerable to a particular activity or task, a new personal risk assessment may be required too.

Incapacity

Unfortunately, there will be occasions when there is no reasonable adjustment or control measure that will enable an employee to return to their original job, in these cases, consider alternative employment.

Access to Work

Many employers do not know that they can claim money for workplace adaptations, such as wheelchair ramps, from the government via Access to Work (ATW) (bit.ly/1Dwc5wK), especially if employing a person with a disability or need to make changes for an employee with a permanent disability.

This is especially useful news for employers with less than 10 staff who can contact the Access to Work service and receive 100% of the costs of equipment/adjustments.

How Much Can You Claim

There is a scale of free money depending on the size of business, see the resources list below to check current allowances and how to qualify.

Great news too; if you have new employees they can claim for Access to Work during the first six weeks of working. Businesses can receive 100% of all approved costs.

If anyone is in need of help in work, he or she can contact Access to Work as soon as possible. If you have an occupational health service, they will work with the employee to make sure that this happens.

Workers will get up to 100% of all approved costs for adaptations if they are:

♦ Currently unemployed and starting a new job
♦ Working for an employer and been in the post for less than six weeks

Mental Health

Remploy (bit.ly/2fwus6B) is the sole provider of the mental health support service for Access to Work. The service provides a range of support for people with mental health conditions for six months and includes:

♦ Work focused psychological health support tailored to each person
♦ Assessment of a person's need for coping strategies
♦ Personalised support plan, detailing the steps required to stay in, or return to work
♦ Advice and guidance to enable employers to fully understand mental health and how they can support employees who have a mental health condition
♦ Identifying reasonable adjustments within the workplace or within the confines of working practice

Further Advice and Resources

♦ A - Z UK Government information (hit.ly/2fvQV3S) and disability advice
♦ Access to Work Guide for Employers (hit.ly/2wUBFnI) with fact sheet

37. Wellbeing

In 2015/16, some 30.4 million working days were lost in the UK due to self-reported work-related illness or injury, with each person taking an average of 16 days off work.

Stress, depression or anxiety together with musculo-skeletal disorders accounted for the majority of days lost due to work-related ill health – 11.7 million days and 8.8 million days respectively.

Many businesses are focusing on health and wellbeing to reduce these figures,. Programmes can range from encouraging staff to take an active interest in their health, to providing support and guidance on specific topics such as nutrition or mindfulness.

Did you know?

- ♦ 1 in 2 people will develop cancer at some point in their lives, according to Cancer Research UK
- ♦ Heart disease is the UK's number one killer
- ♦ Strokes are the third most common cause of death in the UK. Yet in 80% of cases, there are no prior symptoms
- ♦ Heart disease and strokes along with liver and kidney disease often show no warning signs and are sometimes described as 'silent killers'

But taking early action can prevent construction workers developing many of these conditions even though the illnesses may not be work-related. And, whilst there is no law for health checks on wellbeing grounds, nowadays it is considered best practice and as a means of retaining staff.

Overall, the focus on wellbeing is for workers to be well, in good health physically, mentally and emotionally, with a balanced state of mind.

Many employers across the UK already commit to programmes that ensure their workers stay healthy at work instead of those required by law.

Wellbeing services and programmes can be part of an overall package provided by medical support services, such as occupational health (OH), helping organisations to improve performance, through addressing:

♦ Employee's commitment to work
♦ Staff performance and productivity
♦ Staff turnover and intention to leave
♦ Attendance levels
♦ Staff recruitment and retention
♦ Customer satisfaction
♦ Organisational image and reputation
♦ Potential litigation

I mention OH services specifically as many dovetail wellbeing programmes in with the health surveillance programmes. They also have the expertise and understand your workplace and what might be suitable.

The Business Case

The Ashridge/Nuffield Report (bit.ly/2wYKDAz) cites three reasons for investing in wellbeing programmes:

1. Surveys found that when health and wellbeing are actively promoted:
   o The organisation is 2.5 times more likely to be a best performer
   o Employees will be 8 times more likely to engage
   o The organisation is 3.5 times more likely to be creative and innovative
   o The organisation is 4 times less likely to lose talent in the next year
2. Sickness costs an average of £600 per employee per year
3. In companies that had a wellbeing programme, sickness absence was reduced by 82%, and 33% had reduced staff turnover

A successful wellbeing programmes takes planning and organising, well in advance of delivery.

Typical Programmes

Some health promotion activities focus on a single illness or risk factor, such as the prevention of heart disease or trying to change individual behaviour (e.g., smoking or diet). However, health promotions work best as an ongoing process of improving health over time, based on a series of activities rather than one-off initiatives.

Advice usually focuses on identifying goals and objectives for health promotion programmes, ensuring they are cost-effective with the potential for maximum impact with individuals and groups of workers.

Deciding on the right health promotion programme is essential.

In order to get the best results, organisations can ask their workers what they would like:

- What would employees want to change? (Use questionnaires to find out)
- Do the majority of workers smoke? Or are they overweight? (Be sensitive to the feelings of those who do not want to change.)
- Would employees like to increase physical activity, perhaps by cycling to work? (Consider installing bicycle racks, showers, lockers, etc.)
- Who is the target of the programme - office staff, production workers or employees doing a combination of different roles?
- What age are the employees? (Older workers may be more interested in issues such as heart disease and cancers, whilst younger workers may enjoy exercise programmes.)

Health issues	Type of programme	Workers
Heart Disease	Cholesterol testing, stop smoking, blood pressure, diabetes, weight management, benefits of exercise	Ageing, smokers, overweight, office workers, under 20's
Accidents Driving	Speeding, drink/drugs, smoking, planning journeys, defensive driving techniques, road rage, fatigue	Lorry drivers, sales reps, senior executives, delivery drivers, shift workers
Lung health	Smoking, using masks for working, health effects of work on lungs, air pollution, pollen exposure, dealing with asthma, using the correct respiratory protection to prevent lung problems	Young, working with dust, fumes and environmental hazards in the air
Cancers	Smoking, obesity, diet, self-examination, sexual behaviours, sun sense	Outdoor, young, construction, shift workers
General health	Stress management, back care, manual handling, nutrition, weight control, blood pressure, general health check, executive medical, male/female health checks, urine sample for sugar, retirement planning, substance abuse, physical exercise, binge drinking, caffeine, eating habits, sleep, dental care, vision, presenteeism, work/life balance, preventing dehydration, noise exposure, menopause	Executives, management, warehousing, construction, ageing workers

Also, people vary in terms of how they participate in health promotion programmes (e.g., group sessions, one-to-one sessions, poster campaigns, questionnaires, organised events, sponsored charity events).

Regarding the development, implementation, and maintenance of workplace wellbeing and safety initiatives, the interviews from Campbell Institute (bit.ly/2h4Ijy3) participants revealed five key pieces of advice for a successful programme:

1. Pilot health and wellbeing programs with stakeholder input
2. Craft good communication
3. Experiment with incentive structures
4. Organise frequent fitness/wellness competitions
5. Connect wellbeing to safety

Further Advice and Resources

- ◆ Download quizzes and toolkits from the NHS Choices website (bit.ly/1pBKfyH)
- ◆ The calendar of the UK national health promotion campaigns (bit.ly/2wZzhw9) can be found on the NHS Employers website
- ◆ NICE guidance focusing on Productive and Healthy Workplaces
- ◆ Workplace Wellbeing - bridging Health and Safety (bit.ly/2h4Ijy3) from Campbells research (USA)
- ◆ 7 Steps to a Successful Workplace Well-being Programme: (bit.ly/2xybx23)
- ◆ British Heart Foundation resource pages (bit.ly/2xzOST7) for wellbeing programmes and policy templates
- ◆ Fourteen Wellbeing Initiatives (bit.ly/2zK7vSP) from Forbes to boost engagement and productivity

38. Confidentiality and Data Protection

There are general principles under the law regarding the processing of data. Information must be:

♦ Used fairly and lawfully
♦ Used as it should be or as specified
♦ Is not excessive
♦ Destroyed when it is no longer needed, and
♦ Kept safe and secure

Health information requires stronger legal protection; health professionals will apply these principles, plus their own professional code when dealing with workers.

Medical v's Health Records

Any type of health surveillance requires the creation of medical records (occupational health records/case notes). These are entirely separate from the health record as required by the Control of Substances Hazardous to Health (bit.ly/2tQvGeY) as they contain personal health information about the individual, and protected by medical confidentiality.

Further Advice and Resources

- Key definitions (bit.ly/2feXPqS) of the <u>Data Protection Act</u>
- All health professionals follow the principles as set out in their particular code of conduct, an example of which is the <u>guidance issued by the General Medical Council</u> (bit.ly/2rIkqV4)
- To discover what personal data a business can lawfully keep about workers <u>go to the Gov.UK web pages</u> (bit.ly/2ffFdXQ)
- See the <u>full list of guidance available for organisations</u> (bit.ly/2ffO4Zv) from the Information Commissioner's Office
- The new law comes into force from May 2018: <u>The General Data Protection Regulations</u> (bit.ly/2yHGCOL) replaces the DPA. Guidance from the Information Commissioners Office

39. Where to Go for Health Information

It's important when giving information to workers that they receive up to date information from reputable sources.

Setting Up Your Own Company Website Health Page

I suggest setting up a web page of information sources regarding health. Here workers access direct links to health information via a company website or they are aware of where to get information. If you don't have a webpage, write the data into a leaflet or hand-out to give to the workers at induction.

I have been involved in setting up many company websites and suggest the following:

♦ For general health information recommend reputable sites such as NHS Choices (bit.ly/2vo1AzZ) website
♦ How to register with a Doctor (bit.ly/2tzl0kB) find your nearest and then complete a form, available as a download from the site.
♦ How to find a Dentist (bit.ly/2tzkbIx)
♦ How pharmacists can help workers (bit.ly/2yRok0E) with health matters
♦ Advice on where to go for mental health issues such as Mind (bit.ly/2qVxJxG) and the emergency number of the Samaritans (bit.ly/2tzfWgj) as a minimum. Include the telephone number of your company counselling services and the free counselling service for construction workers - Lighthouse Charity (bit.ly/2tzpZC8)

Access to health and safety policy documents, especially:

- General statement of health and wellbeing
- Drug and alcohol short statement or policy, setting out expectations and consequences
- Responsibilities of workers such as reporting incidents and complying with company policy
- Display Screen Equipment set up
- Sickness reporting

Other

- An online induction programme to cover the basic safety information and the role of occupational health or other health services
- The types of hazards and risks on site
- Information and expectations about personal protective equipment
- Who to contact in an emergency
- Basic first aid advice, electric shock and if you have an AED, First Aiders
- Sun advice and provision of sunscreens
- Skincare (handwashing, after work creams)
- Welfare facilities and information about food availability
- How to access occupational or medical services
- Vaccinations needed - Weil's disease, tetanus, Hepatitis B and how to get them
- A list of local walk-in treatment and dental centres

Internet Access

- Many sites have banned the use of mobile phones on sites as it is dangerous to be talking on the phone around heavy plant.
- If you do not have your own website, it is easy to set up a page on one of your contractor's sites; here workers log in with their own password
- Make computers available for workers
- The HSE has a number of leaflets in different languages or use Google Translate (bit.ly/2tzAbdW)
- Mobile phone apps are available, for example, look at this British Red Cross First Aid (bit.ly/2tzzhOv) app or why not make your own?
- HSE free 'talking leaflets' (bit.ly/2xzCUso) some general leaflets

40. Toolbox Talks

A 'toolbox talk' is a short presentation to the workforce on a single aspect of health and safety. Toolbox talks are a useful way of keeping health and safety at the forefront of your team's minds and making them aware of the current risks and hazards on a single aspect of health and safety.

They can be simple discussions, a presentation or video.

The Best Tool Box Talks are:

What	How
Relevant:	Make sure the talk is about issues on your worksite and work you do, personalise the talk to the team you talk to
In the right place:	Give the talk where the workers can fully concentrate on your message
Include stories:	Tell a real story, an example of why this talk is essential to make the issue more real
Improved:	Listen and act on feedback for the next talk
Brief:	Focus on a single topic
Engaging:	Make the talk interactive and encourage participation, for example, set a problem and ask for solutions
Controlled:	Manage the meeting so that everyone is focused on the subject and keep discussions relevant

How to Do a Great Tool Box Talk

- ♦ Workers pay more attention if the talk is from an experienced, respected and trusted worker rather than a book-trained teacher with no experience
- ♦ Most people underestimate the risks they take on the job. Getting people to think about the dangers makes a situation more real

- Be enthusiastic and deliver a clear message about the importance of the topic
- Know the audience. If workers don't understand English think how to get the messages across
- Keep it simple. Use short, straightforward words and phrases avoiding slang or jargon
- Respect your audience and listen to their views
- Use the right tone of voice
- Do not rush the presentation
- Use open questions, rather than questions people just answer 'yes' or 'no' to
- Some topics may need more of an explanation than others. Do not be impatient
- Keep positive. Focus on what people can do to create a safe working environment and not the negatives

And remember - toolbox talks prevent accidents or incidents – but you may never know if it did!

Safety Alerts

These are short guidance notes that highlight an incident or unsafe practice, sent out quickly to alert people about an issue and prevent similar events. They usually contain immediate actions or a message to spread best practice. Most are communicated by email, text messages, a company website page or newsletter.

Further Advice and Resources

- To see some examples of safety alerts go to the Southern Shield website (bit.ly/2rcbweY)
- The HSE have examples of toolbox talks (bit.ly/2rcgfgB)

41. Tendering for Work/Contracts

Rules of Tendering

An important part of any construction company's' life is getting work; there are many ways of doing this.

This section focuses on the health and wellbeing aspects of tender applications and advice on what to include:

What to Include
Provide evidence of any claims you make such as photographs of facilities provided, policy, and completed audits of compliance with your health surveillance programmes or health promotion materials.
Do not add everything in one big download or information dump; far from impressing it demonstrates that you do not understand the brief.
Consider the contract you are tendering for and suggest ways to improve delivery or cutting costs.
Include testimonials or successes from recent projects.
Actively involve your health and safety professionals in looking at the specification - do not try to do it all yourself
Suggest ways you have worked before on similar projects.
For all procedures/policy cite industry-wide references to support your suggestion, e.g. HSE reports, NICE guidance, CBH standards
If in doubt, do not hesitate to go back to the client to clarify points.

Client Decision-Making Process

Winning tenders is a costly business - the client is looking for value, and this often means adding more than required in order to outbid your opponents.

When assessing a health proposal in a bid, the rules are:

1. Does the application meet the required standard?
2. Is it of a higher standard than required?
3. Is it innovative and flexible and likely to exceed expectations?
4. Do the tenderers understand what we are asking for? This will come out in the language you use and the terminology. This is why it is essential to have a health professional's input.

I know this will vary from company to company, but I use the five categories of scoring:

1. Has not met any of the objectives
2. Met some of the objectives
3. Met all objectives
4. Over delivered on objectives
5. Gone beyond the objectives and aims to achieve a comprehensive response

Also considered is the cost or cost savings of each recommendation made. Companies will have their own view of how cost (quality versus quantity) impact on awarding contracts. Many go with the lowest price. But that is not always the best way forward for some services, especially when considering say medical services for your sites, and one would look at the quality of the processes described (e.g. response time, reports, IT services, economies of scale, facilities) for a full picture.

The Assessment Process

Usually, a number of reviewers assess the bids. Each reviewer takes away a scoring card and sets a score using their professional skills to assess each suggestion against each objective set by the client. Hopefully, everyone will come to the same conclusion, and there will be an outright winner.

The most significant issue I have come across when assessing the provision of medical services, is that many believe occupational health OH) is about health and well-being (checking blood pressures and measuring cholesterol); but it's not. OH is about protecting workers health, so it's crucial that this is set out and a priority in your proposal.

Without understanding the true nature of OH, work, and employers or principal contractor's duties under law, the bid is almost guaranteed not to meet the standard required.

If there are two or even three bidders who are close in terms of quality and price, you could be asked to present your findings to key stakeholders before a final decision is made.

Further Advice and Resources

- ♦ How to tender for public sector contracts (bit.ly/2s5xi4g)
- ♦ Writing a PPQ for Construction (bit.ly/2xLNDjF) with video

42. Maturity Index for Construction

Have you ever wondered how you are doing in terms of workplace health protection compared to other construction companies? If so, you can measure your compliance by filling in the maturity index tool, created by the HSE for construction companies. It is a series of questions covering subjects such as leadership, business beliefs, fairness, mindfulness, etc. These topics are subdivided into further sections.

For example:

There is a section labelled 'Business Beliefs'; this is subdivided into a further three categories of:

1. 'Good health is good business.'
2. Occupational health risk management
3. Occupational health is a core business value

In each of the three are some statements that you can agree or disagree with by rating your own business. You can choose one of five responses ranging from A (not good) to E (Excellent).

Your completed responses generate your own personal company report, which provides a plan on where you need to focus on in the future.

Further Advice and Resources

- ◆ For more information go to <u>HSL Maturity Index Questionnaire</u> (bit.ly/2rchtIQ)
- ◆ Read the full research paper on the <u>HSE Maturity Index development</u> (bit.ly/2rck2dL)

43. Retaining Your Workforce

There are 2.1 million workers in construction, and, despite occasional drops caused by recessions, employment figures have remained constant over the last decade. As a proportion of the UK labour market as a whole, the percentage of construction jobs has varied slightly since 2005, falling by nearly 1%.

Things are changing, as issues such as ageing, skills shortage and health mean that there are difficulties in recruiting and keeping your workforce. This section looks at these issues in detail and suggests proactive ways of preventing workers leaving.

43.1 The Older Worker

It is reported that 30% of workers are over the age of 50 in construction and with the problem of general ill health as well Construction News (bit.ly/2tzt6tT) agrees that retaining an ageing workforce is a challenge for all industries, and particularly important in construction.

Data shows that nearly 30 percent of men aged 45 will have left the construction industry by the time they hit 50. The average for all other sectors is just 2 percent.

The construction industry is already relying heavily on ageing workers, but there are advantages. Studies show that older workers are more dedicated to the workplace, have fewer sickness absences and stay in jobs longer. The skills, experience and maturity of older workers generally outweigh potential problems such as increasing, age-related ill health.

But an ageing workforce calls for innovation in:

- Health promotion and health education
- Preventing work-related accidents and diseases
- Rehabilitation programmes to get workers back to work early
- Better support for disabled workers

♦ Considering work ability rather than disability

Characteristics of older workers

On the plus side older workers generally:

♦ Are typically wiser, think strategically and consider all angles
♦ Will often take time to think about a situation before acting impulsively
♦ Have more experience and expertise that accumulates with age
♦ Are more suited to the changing face of today's workplace

having good people-skills, customer service, and quality awareness.

Myths

There is no consistent evidence that older workers are generally less productive than younger workers. At the same time, there is accumulating evidence that job experience is a more valid and reliable predictor of productivity than chronological age. Also, mental ability does not generally show any marked decline until after the age of 70.

Accidents

Older workers are generally less likely to have accidents than younger workers, but if they do, it could result in a more serious injury (i.e., permanent disability, or death)

Work-related stress

- ◆ Lack of opportunities for career development and training
- ◆ Difficulties in adapting to changing technologies.

It is not the same for everyone; individual differences in lifestyle, nutrition, fitness, genetic predisposition to illness, educational level, and the work itself will have an impact on how a worker works.

Strategies for Ageing Workers

Age-sensitive risk assessment means taking into account age-related aspects of different age groups when assessing risk, including potential changes in functional capacity and health status in the case of older workers.

Health

A government survey of men aged 50 – 64 across the country, asked why they had left their last job.

In construction, 46 percent said it was because of ill health. This was significantly higher than in any other sector, including other manual and skilled areas such as mining and agriculture. The average across all industries for men retiring for health reasons was just 25 percent.[12]

Health Promotion

Workers of all ages can delay health problems by adopting healthy lifestyle habits, such as regular exercise and healthy eating and the workplace has a pivotal role to play in promoting a healthy lifestyle and supporting activities that encourage workers to become more robust.

Workplace health promotion covers a variety of topics including diet and nutrition, alcohol consumption, quitting smoking, getting enough exercise, recovery and sleep.

Job re-design

Due to substantial individual differences, the way in which the workplace is modified to address changes in functional capacity has to be tailored to the needs and condition of each worker. Good workplace design benefits all age groups while targeting older workers.

Reduce physical capacity by:

- Use of equipment and other assistive technologies
- Restrictions on heavy lifting and physically demanding tasks
- Training in appropriate lifting and carrying techniques
- Proper ergonomic design of tools, equipment and furniture
- Good workplace design to minimise the likelihood of falls

---

[12] Leaders 'shocked' by CN's mental health findings. [online] Construction News. Available at: *bit.ly/2porMeo* Jul. 2017].

Add-ons

- Physiotherapy
- Employee assistance programmes (See Chapter 34, Other Professional Health Services)

Specific age-related conditions

A few factors warrant a special mention

- Musculoskeletal disorders are the most prevalent cause of work disability among older workers
- Chronic symptoms and diseases often impair the ability to work, and a worker returning after a prolonged absence often faces the problem of unchanged work and working conditions
- Menopause guidance from Unison

Results show older people are happy to work longer when they are helped to do so. Research indicates that there are definite benefits to companies who employ them; with lower rates of sick leave, lower work disability costs and better productivity.

43.2 Young Workers

The Law

Children below the minimum school leaving age must not be employed on construction sites, except when on work experience. In addition, under 18's are not allowed to work after 10pm or before 7am. In specified industries such as agriculture and retail, they cannot work from midnight to 4 am. Construction is not such an exemption.

Under the <u>Management of Health and Safety at Work Regulations</u> (bit.ly/2qVrQAJ), an employer has a responsibility to ensure that young people are not exposed to risk due to:

♦ Lack of experience
♦ Being unaware of existing or potential risks and/or
♦ Lack of maturity

An employer must consider:

♦ The layout of the workplace
♦ The physical, biological and chemical agents in the workplace
♦ Handling work equipment
♦ The organisation of work and processes
♦ Health and safety training

Further Advice and Resources

♦ <u>HSE website about young persons</u> (bit.ly/2rjPEhS) the law and responsibilities
♦ <u>ACAS employing young workers</u> (bit.ly/2rjlAmu) with comprehensive guidance on all aspects of employment
♦ Frequently asked questions about young person at work <u>HSE FAQ pages</u> (bit.ly/2rjHhD3)
♦ <u>Apprenticeship funding guide from CITB</u> (bit.ly/2rcffJB)

43.3 Skills

There are issues with a skill shortage too. Employers fear there aren't enough bricklayers, plumbers and project managers coming through to replace those who leave.

Skills Facts

♦ A report by the <u>Recruitment and Employment Confederation (REC)</u> (bit.ly/2xyAri4) describes the skill shortage in construction and engineering as 'critical'.

- And, although the numbers of job opportunities are rising, the number of suitable candidates isn't. The <u>Construction Industry Training Board (CITB)</u> (bit.ly/2xzTiJH) estimates more than 36,000 new workers a year are needed to cover current demand, with recruiters finding it already challenging to cover vacancies.
- The <u>Royal Institute of Chartered Surveyors (RICS)</u> (bit.ly/2xzU1up) has predicted that lack of skills could affect 27,000 construction projects each year until 2019. The RICS survey also showed that 66% of surveying firms have already turned down work due to a lack of staff and this could be set to grow over the next five years.[13]

43.4 Brexit

Will our exit from the UK mean we will not have younger migrant workers to rely on? As of the time of writing (May 2017), one in eight construction workers in the UK is foreign. In London, that figure is 23 percent.

Further Advice and Resources

- The <u>Health and Safety migrant</u> workers website (bit.ly/2qUWUQO) has resources and guidance for managers and covers issues such as:
  - The law
  - Interpreters and translators
  - Site induction
  - English language training schemes
  - Avoiding or minimising racism
- There are many useful apps to translate documents available; I use <u>Google Translate</u> (bit.ly/2qVbeJa), available free for all types of devices
- Unison: <u>Menopause at Work</u> (bit.ly/2o6Bwaf)

---

[13] Beta.agencycentral.co.uk. (2017). Is there a skill shortage in the Construction Industry?. [online] Accessed 25 Jul. 2017.

Before You Go...

I hope you found this book useful and informative. If you have any suggestions on how I can improve, please contact me via my website at www.workingwellsolutions.com

You might also want to look at my other publications such as:

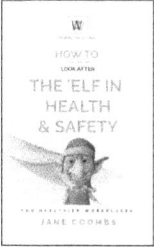

How to Look After the 'Elf in Health and Safety (amzn.to/2sl2Fez) - all about health in many different workplaces for HR, managers and safety professionals

The Manager's Ultimate Guide to Health and Wellbeing at Work (amzn.to/2skuwMe) - everything you wanted to know about health management, practical and realistic advice for workplaces.

If you are interested in what goes on behind locked doors in occupational health and read true, fascinating and sometimes downright dishonest workplace health and safety stories: The Good, the Bad and the Smugly: Behind the Scenes in Occupational Health (amzn.to/2toZLSL)

Finally, if you have enjoyed this book, it would really help spread the word, if you could give me an honest review from wherever you purchased it.

I really want to make a difference to workplace health and these books contain all the information to do just that

Thankyou - Jane (February 2018)

Appendix 1: Construction Resources

	Organisation	Short link
ACAS	The Advisory, Conciliation and Arbitration Service	bit.ly/2r6t38e
Access to Work	Disability - help with adaptations	bit.ly/2foeKui
B&CE	Improving financial welfare of those in construction	bit.ly/2fmjYqm
British Occupational Hygiene Society	Scientific assessment of health risks on site	bit.ly/1Hio449
British Safety Council		bit.ly/2fofZJY
British Standards	Online shop	bit.ly/2foomlY
BSG	Building Safety Group	bit.ly/2fnDrqQ
C.O.N.I.A.C	Construction Industry Advisory Committee	bit.ly/2qqi9se
Chartered Society of Physiotherapists	Chartered Society of Physiotherapists	bit.ly/2r6O4ji
CITA	Construction IT Alliance	bit.ly/2fnD9jy
CITB	Construction Industry Training Board	bit.ly/2xzTiJH
CLOC	Construction Logistics and Community Safety	bit.ly/2fnBCtM
CCS	Considerate Construction Scheme	bit.ly/2fnjbWr
CBH	Constructing Better Health	bit.ly/2tQv7Sg

Construction News	Industry Magazine	bit.ly/2r6lpuL
Construction Sector - HSE website	Information and free guidance	bit.ly/2fmjDnA
Counselling and Debt advice services	Employee Assistance Programmes	bit.ly/2qpZpct
CSCS	Construction Skills Certification Scheme	bit.ly/2fo1JRA
Designing Buildings WIKI	Construction industry knowledge base, website	bit.ly/2fn92ZO
DVLA	Medical Standards for Drivers	bit.ly/2r6b0PK
EA	Environment Agency	bit.ly/2qW6SBK
FOM	Faculty of Occupational Medicine	bit.ly/2fpjO1v
Fit for Work Scheme	Government guidance	bit.ly/2gEJxDB
Government contracts finder	For contracts over £100K	bit.ly/2fo0HFg
Health and Safety in Construction ACOP	HSG 150 from the HSE	bit.ly/2fnQXe9
Health in Construction Group	Leadership Group Website	bit.ly/2qq71fh
Highways England	Roads	bit.ly/2qVFmnI
Lighthouse Charity	Free, confidential EAP and counselling	bit.ly/2tzpZC8
Managing Mental Health	Business in the Community Toolkit	bit.ly/2qqcrH3
Managing Occupational Health	Free Guidance from IOSH	bit.ly/2ljLbr1

Managing Suicide	Business in the Community Toolkit	bit.ly/2qq2NEd
Medical Fitness for Plant Operations	Construction Plant Hire Association	bit.ly/2fnLELu
Mental Health First Aid	Line Managers Toolkit	bit.ly/2fpnSyN
MIND	For better mental health	bit.ly/2qVxJxG
NMC	Nurses Registration Body	bit.ly/2fnFZVX
Office of Rail Regulation	Rail and Road Users protection	www.orr.gov.uk
OH Maturity Index	Health and Safety Laboratory	bit.ly/2rchtIQ
Responsibility Deal Construction Pledge		bit.ly/1MxJoYE
RICS	Royal Institute of Chartered Surveyors	bit.ly/2xzU1up
RoSPA	Royal Society for Prevention of Accidents	bit.ly/2fmy6Ac
SEQOHS	Safe Effective Quality Occupational Health Services	bit.ly/2fnkdSl
Samaritans	Emergency help and support	bit.ly/2fn4fr6
Working Well Together	Construction Industry Awareness	wwt.uk.com/
Working Well Solutions	Jane Coombs website for Occ Health and safety	bit.ly/wws-com

Appendix 2: Absence Resources

	Short Link	Notes
Access to Work Guide	bit.ly/2wUBFnI	Funding for workplace adjustments
Bradford Index to Manage Absence	bit.ly/2wUjKh2	Working Well Solutions article
Employer Help book for Statutory Sick Pay	bit.ly/2wUYmbz	HM Revenue and Customs
Employers Direct	bit.ly/2tsLCDX	Free legal advice for UK businesses
Equality Act guidance	bit.ly/2ttDKCe	Disability advice for workplaces
Fit for work service help sheets	bit.ly/2gEJxDB	Gov. UK fact sheets
Fit for Work service	bit.ly/2vBzfGT	Scotland 0800 019 2211 (free)
Fit for Work service	bit.ly/2vBKFdH	England and Wales 0800 032 6235 (free)
Is it a health or safety hazard?	bit.ly/2ttgC6G	Working Well Solutions article
Long-term sickness absence and incapacity	bit.ly/2h2DdC5	NICE Guidance
Manager Guide: Phased Return to Work	bit.ly/2ttc9AY	Working Well Solutions article
Manager's guide to managing absence	bit.ly/2wULBhj	Working Well Solutions article

Managing for Health and Safety	bit.ly/2tsX2HN	HSE guidance
Recovering from Surgery	bit.ly/2tQtpR4	Royal College of Surgeons lists of recovery times
Requesting a formal referral to OH	bit.ly/2wUeOZn	Working Well Solutions article
Return to Work After Sickness Absence	bit.ly/2wUot2h	CIPD
Return to Work Interviews	bit.ly/2uNeDhh	Working Well Solutions video
Risk Assessment	bit.ly/2tQbTw9	Guidance from HSE
Sick and holiday pay	bit.ly/2wUDsct	ACAS article
Sickness absence	bit.ly/2wUyJYa	HSE general information
Statutory sick pay, employer guide	bit.ly/2tsM98V	UK government
What is occupational health (video)	bit.ly/2wUEwwZ	Working Well Solutions

About the Author

I qualified as a general nurse until I decided that factories, foundries and construction sites were far more interesting. Having to deal with the working well was challenging and a way of preventing ill health rather than having to pick up the pieces in casualty and the operating theatres of Guys Hospital.

After qualifying I started at the Ford Motor Company and had a series of jobs ranging from manufacturing, local government and private occupational health providers. On the way, I gained more professional qualifications in health and an MSC in Occupational Health, Safety and Environmental Management.

Now I have become more involved with UK Construction; working with the HSE and various consultative groups on many of the health issues, such as fitness for work on plant and controlling construction dust. I have also drafted guidance for IOSH and the HSE.

I have run my own consultancy business - Working Well Solutions Ltd (bit.ly/wws-com)

I am married and has five grown up independent children. I lives on the south coast where I runs my own website and advises callers and companies on all aspects of occupational health and safety. I am also working towards a Masters in creative writing.

If you would like to keep in contact with me and hear about the latest news of workplace health why not follow me or give me a thumbs up?

Twitter - (bit.ly/1pIzpDM): @WWSOccHealth

LinkedIn - (bit.ly/2nThhxA): https://www.linkedin.com/in/jane-coombs-wws

Facebook - (bit.ly/2nS3pDY): @WorkingWellSolutions

Or visit my website (bit.ly/wws-com) to join my mailing list, download free resources, read my blog or email jane.coombs@workingwellsolutions.com.

www.ingramcontent.com/pod-product-compliance
Lightning Source LLC
Chambersburg PA
CBHW060551200326
41521CB00007B/553